Whether you're older and "cramming for finals" or think of death as a far-distant prospect, the statistic is still the same: to wit, one out of one. This book will make you think about death. But that sounds so depressing, and this is not a depressing book. You will like it! If you're a believer, it will cause you to look forward to "home," and, if not, you will want to.

Stephen Brown, Professor
Reformed Theological Seminary, Orlando
Radio Bible Teacher on Key Life

This is one of the most important and compelling books I have ever read. Larry Dixon's conversational style in dealing with inescapable eternal realities makes this a serious page-turner. A must read for those who are ready for heaven and for those who are not. Practical. Convicting.

Terry Hulbert, Professor of Bible Exposition
Columbia Biblical Seminary and School of Missions

It's about time that someone is willing to talk about heaven . . . for heaven's sake! Larry Dixon knows his subject well and is uniquely qualified to write about heaven. Ponder it! Reflect upon it! Then share it with someone who needs to be there!

David Olshine, Director
Youth Ministries Program
Columbia International University

Larry Dixon has written a very encouraging and hopeful book. Full of genuine theological insight, it nevertheless addresses the reader without theological training; while technically insightful, it does not get encumbered with technical issues and technical language. I recommend it for the new Christian who wishes to get in touch with the hope of the Christian life, and for the longtime believer who wants deeper insight into the issues of Christian hope. Dixon has written a book that is good for all of us.

A.J. (Chip) Conyers, Professor of Theology
George W. Truett Theological Seminary/Baylor University
Author, *The Eclipse of Heaven*

Larry Dixon helps his readers to avoid the profound and distressing sense of meaninglessness which inevitably sets in when we realize that even accomplishing most of our earthly goals will not/cannot bring us to heaven. . . . Only God in Christ can do that.

Stephen Farra, Director
Psychology Program
Columbia International University

Professor Dixon has written an engaging, practically applicable and biblically based treatment of the Christian's blessed hope. I especially appreciate the way in which he exposes the many erroneous views of the afterlife prevalent in contemporary culture. This book is a fitting sequel to his excellent work on the doctrine of eternal punishment entitled The Other Side of the Good News. *I recommend both of these books to Christians wishing to receive solid teaching on the eternal state.*

Alan W. Gomes, Associate Professor and Chair
Department of Theology
Talbot School of Theology

HEAVEN:

Thinking Now About Forever

Larry Dixon

CHRISTIAN PUBLICATIONS, INC.
CAMP HILL, PENNSYLVANIA

Dedication

This study of heaven is fondly dedicated to
Dr. Kenneth Mulholland, my academic dean—
and friend—at Columbia Biblical Seminary
and School of Missions. Thanks, Ken, for your
example of one who models a life lived in light of eternity.

⊞ CHRISTIAN PUBLICATIONS, INC.
3825 Hartzdale Drive, Camp Hill, PA 17011
www.christianpublications.com

Heaven: Thinking Now About Forever
ISBN: 0-88965-182-5
© 2002 by Larry Dixon
All rights reserved
Printed in the United States of America

02   03   04   05   06   5   4   3   2   1

C O N T E N T S

Foreword vii

Introduction 1

1 Imagine There's No Heaven..7

2 Hijacked to Paradise 21

3 Wrong Thoughts of Heaven...37

4 Heaven Only Knows!...53

5 Better than Baxter:
  A Brief Survey of the Bible on Heaven...............................65

6 Heaven Came Down..87

7 Endless *Inactivity*?..103

8 For Heaven's Sake! 139

Endnotes..167

Scripture References Index..177

Foreword

When life here on earth was hard for Christian people, the hope of glory glowed in their minds, and they were frank in proclaiming what they knew about heaven and declaring how much they looked forward to it. Evidence of this comes from the hymns and devotional writings of the patristic, medieval, reformational, Puritan, historic evangelical and black American constituencies, all of which in this respect were directly tuned in to the future-oriented wavelength of the New Testament.

Today, however, things are different. Now that life in the West has become affluent, comfortable, and entertainment-oriented for most people, including most churchgoers, the focus of interest has shifted to celebrating what we receive from God in this life, and the doctrine of the hereafter has become in key respects unvisited and unmapped territory. Beyond question, this has brought major loss. It is one of the reasons why, compared to our evangelical ancestors and to contemporary Christians in many other parts of the world, we often appear as a generation of worldly wimps.

Larry Dixon's exploration of elements of the New Testament witness to heaven is marked by biblical faithfulness and easy lucidity, not to mention a humane sense of humor. It is a book in season, dispelling some of the fog about heaven and letting the light shine through. It will surely do good.

J.I. Packer
Regent College,
Vancouver, BC

Introduction

My first book, *The Other Side of the Good News*,[1] an in-depth discussion of the difficult doctrine of hell, was honestly hard to write. It seemed to me, however, that in the face of the evangelical "overhaul" of hell, the contemporary exodus from the clear teaching of the bad news of the good news, as given by the Good Shepherd Himself, necessitated a response.

That response may not have answered all the questions raised by those whose viewpoints differ from what Jesus taught about the fate of the wicked. Hell, of course, is no delightful doctrine; one should weep when discussing the destiny of what appears to be the majority of the human race.

Not so a discussion of heaven! The believer in Jesus Christ today is not handicapped by thinking about that subject too much—he thinks about it far too little. A past generation was accused of being so "heavenly-minded that they were of no earthly good." Hardly can the same be said about today's Christians. We are more apt not to be "minded" about anything, much less where we will spend eternity. For so many in our complex times, managing day to day is the primary issue, not imagining what that next world will entail. "Setting one's mind on heaven," the Apostle Paul's God-inspired admonition to the believer, seems to apply only to Christian retirees who are waiting to "go home to be with the Lord" or to preachers who are preparing a sermon series on the Second Coming.

You may have heard the story of Sherlock Holmes and Dr. Watson going on a camping trip. After a good meal, they lay down for the night, and went to sleep. Some hours later, Holmes awoke and nudged his faithful friend. "Watson, look up at the sky and tell me what you see."

Watson replied, "I see millions and millions of stars."

"What does that tell you?" Holmes asked.

Watson pondered for a minute. "Astronomically, it tells me that there are millions of galaxies and potentially billions of planets. Astrologically, I observe that Saturn is in Leo. Chronologically, I deduce that the time is approximately a quarter past three. Theologically, I can see that God is all-powerful and that we are small and insignificant. Meteorologically, I suspect that we will have a beautiful day tomorrow. What does it tell you, Holmes?"

Holmes was silent for a minute, then spoke. "Watson, you idiot! It tells me that somebody has stolen our tent!"

To a great degree, we are as clueless as Watson. Someone has stolen heaven—or at least its appeal—from Christians! We must discuss the topic of heaven—and the making of preparations to go there—for at least three reasons which present themselves in Scripture.

The first is that *the hope of heaven should motivate the believer to godliness*. The study of final things (eschatology) should not lead to battles among believers, nor to personal complacency, but to purity in the people of God. John argues in First John 3:1-3 that Christ will one day appear, and "we shall be like him, for we shall see him as he is." What medieval theologians referred to as the "beatific vision" (seeing God face to face) John sets forth as the completing stage of the believer's sanctification. One who looks upon the Son of God will become like the Son of God.

Rather than leading the believer to inactive sky-gazing, like the disciples at Christ's ascension (Acts 1:11), John emphasizes that the hope of seeing the Lord as He is ought to lead to personal purity: "Everyone who has this hope in him purifies himself, just as he is pure" (1 John 3:3). The contemplation of our yet-to-be-realized hope in heaven should motivate us to active and aggressive cooperation in our sanctification right now.

The second reason for the study of heaven is that *it ought to motivate the believer to service.* Our poor concepts of heaven understandably bore believers and repel the unrepentant. Why should we be surprised that unbelievers turn away from the gospel when we often act as if heaven is a place of endless harp-strumming with the angels? The late evangelist Paul Little said that the angels have a "pep rally" over every sinner who repents (Luke 15:10). How dare we imply that there will be less excitement when those sinners are finally in the presence of the Savior who died for them?

If we understand heaven to be the absolute perfection of all our dreams and God-honoring desires, then we will work in light of that certainty. We make a grave evangelistic error when we cause unbelievers to think that heaven will be just like our church services—only *l-o-n-g-e-r.* I must admit that I'm fairly anxious to see the noon hour come on Sunday so I can go home—and *I'm the preacher!*

As I argued in my first book, the certainty of hell for those who reject Jesus Christ ought to motivate the Christian to join the rescue squad. Similarly, the assured hope of heaven ought to joyfully drive the disciple of Christ to go into the highways and by-ways of life, and compel unbelievers to come in (Luke 14:23). The King is not like an expensive restaurant's maitre d' whose palm must be greased before he grudgingly grants a table, and that near the kitchen. The heavenly King wants his banquet overflowing with guests. Tony Campolo certainly has the right idea when he suggests that "the kingdom of God is a party!"

The third reason for this study is that *the hope of heaven ought to bring the believer to worship*. Our concept of heaven will inevitably flow from our concept of God and his majesty. If we envision God as only a Resident Policeman, to use one of J.B. Phillips' designations,[2] One who looks to flatten people who might be having fun, then heaven will appear to be an eternity of somberness and restrictions. If we understand God as a doting, almost senile Grand Old Man,[3] then heaven might conjure up images in our minds of elderly nursing home patients playing checkers in the community room.

If, however, we understand God to be the One "with eternal pleasures at [His] right hand" (Psalm 16:11), the One who aggressively seeks worshipers (John 4:23), and the One whom Dorothy Sayers says never bored a soul in thirty-three years, then heaven takes on an attractiveness which can hardly be resisted. How sad not to long to see the One who died for unworthy, hell-bound sinners! And how pitiful not to strive for that moment when "we shall be like him, for we shall see him as he is" (1 John 3:2). If we contemplated the glories of heaven more, would we not focus on Him who makes heaven glorious? *He* is its attraction, not pearly gates, nor streets of gold, nor the prospect of no more pain.

We sometimes speak of "getting up on the wrong side of the bed," of being "on the wrong side of the law," of being born "on the wrong side of the tracks." There is, indeed, a right side and a wrong side of the gospel. There are no fence-sitters when it comes to the gospel of Jesus Christ.

One is either on His side or living in opposition to Him. Those who are on the wrong side of the gospel need to be warned; those who by grace have been brought onto the right side of the good news need to be reminded of what awaits them after this life.

With this justification in place, we begin. And our prayer is that such an investigation of the right side of the good news will indeed move us to become more ardent disciples of Jesus Christ, more burdened for the lost, and more accurate and eager worshipers of the One who is the focal point of heaven. Are you ready to get ready?

ONE

Imagine There's No Heaven

I can swear there ain't no heaven
But I pray there ain't no hell.
But I'll never know by livin'
Only my dyin' will tell.

(Blood, Sweat and Tears' "And When I Die")

Imagine there's no heaven
It's easy if you try;
No hell below us,
Above us only sky.

(John Lennon's "Imagine")

There is a way that seems right to a man, but in the end it leads to death.

(Proverbs 14:12)

My, how we speak so cavalierly of heaven! "Thank Heaven for Seven-Eleven!" gushed one ad several years ago. We express surprise by "Oh, my heavens!" or "What in heaven's name!" or "Heavens to Betsy!" (I still don't get that one. Who *is* this Betsy, and what's she got to do with heaven?)

An appeal to get one out of a jam might be expressed by "Heaven help us!" When a mystery is unable to be unlocked by human intelligence we might say, "Heaven only knows!" We have a flavor of ice cream called "Heavenly Hash" and a perfume named "Heaven-Sent" (which may have given rise to the expression, "stinks to high heaven!").

I must admit I am guilty of misusing the term myself on occasion. When one of my teaching friends is on his way to class, I might encourage him with the words, "Give 'em heaven!"

Human romantic love seems to be the highest experience one can hope for in a heaven-less world. The song "Almost Paradise" describes a romance between two people in terms of "knocking on heaven's door."[1] Country music star Shania Twain's hit "You Win My Love," speaks of giving away one's "soul" to another human who "makes my motor run."[2]

How sad. "Heaven" has become a metaphor for a superior sexual encounter. If by "soul" Twain means that immortal part of us which survives death (and it seems that is indeed what she means), then this love-song is a sad exercise in idolatry. Only *God* should get our soul, our heart, our all.

There are many books which have "heaven" in the title—and not all of them are cheap romances! Maria Shriver has written a children's book entitled *What's Heaven?* Raised Catholic, she writes that heaven "is a beautiful place up in the sky, where no one is sick, where no one is mean or unhappy. It's a place beyond the moon, the stars, and the clouds. . . . Heaven isn't a place you can see. . . . It's somewhere you believe in."[3]

Worse Than Heaven's Trivialization

What could be worse than the trivialization of heaven? How about imagining its non-existence? That's precisely what the late John Lennon suggested in his song "Imagine." He wrote that we should "imagine there's no heaven," telling us that to think heaven (and hell) out of existence would help us live for today and live as one.[4]

That song was nine years old when something terrible occurred in 1980. At the age of forty, John Lennon had no reason to suspect that, hours after signing a fan's record album, the young autograph-seeker would assume a combat stance outside Lennon's Manhattan apartment building and pump at least four bullets into him. Thus Mark David Chapman ended the life of the creative force behind the most successful musical group in history, the Beatles.

Sean, Yoko Ono and Lennon's five-year-old son, asked his mother simple questions about the man who calmly cut down his father. "If he liked him so much, why did he kill him?" His mother said that the killer was confused and his fate would be decided by the courts. "Which court are you talking about?" Sean asked. "Basketball or tennis?" He then cried and said, "Now Daddy is part of God. I guess when you die you become much bigger because you're part of everything."[5] One mourner left a wreath of flowers in front of the Dakota building. It read, "Christmas in Heaven."

Lennon as Lord?

If we analyze the words to Lennon's song "Imagine," we discover that the mourner who laid that particular wreath failed to grasp Lennon's perspective on the afterlife. Leaving an estate of $235 million, this was the member of the Beatles who said in a 1966 interview with British journalist Maureen Cleave that, "Christianity will go. It will vanish and shrink. I needn't argue that; I'm right and I will be proved right. We're more popular than Jesus now."[6]

One Lennon devoteé on the Internet reports that Chapman was driven to murder Lennon specifically because of those comments he made in 1966 about Jesus. Paul McCartney later evaluated Lennon's remarks about Christianity by saying, "Was it a mistake? I don't know. In the short term yeah, maybe not in the long term." The same Internet fan mentioned above regards Lennon as the "world's most respected Martyr" and states that the song "Imagine" is "probably the one song most revealing of his deity."[7]

How sad. A close look at the words of Lennon's song shows that he was correct in stating that it is easy, at least for many, to imagine there's no heaven. And it is certainly desirable to most people to imagine that there is "no hell below us, above us only sky." The song's theme seems to be that people are not "livin' for today" because the belief in heaven keeps the world from living as one.

But Lennon's song does not pick only on Christian faith. The second stanza suggests that we should dispense with national loyalties, for then there would be "nothing to kill or die for." Religion in general (not just Christianity) should be discarded and all the people would "live in peace."

Catastrophic Conclusions

Let's take Lennon's perspective for a few moments and imagine there's no heaven. If we look at one of the key passages concerning heaven which is given by Jesus, certain conclusions are undeniable. In John 14:1-3 Jesus says,

> Do not let your hearts be troubled. Trust in God;
> trust also in me. In my Father's house are many

rooms; if it were not so, I would have told you. I
am going there to prepare a place for you. And if I
go and prepare a place for you, I will come back
and take you to be with me that you also may be
where I am.

If the words of John Lennon are to be followed, if there
is indeed no heaven, three very clear conclusions can be
drawn about this passage:

First, *we have no reason to trust in God* (verse 1). Jesus
says to His disciples, "Do not let your hearts be troubled.
Trust in God; trust also in me." But if there is no afterlife,
why be troubled about religion at all? If there is no heaven,
there is likely no God either. Why, indeed, would one
worry about a God who has application only to this brief,
earthly life? How can one "trust in God" when He has not
told us the truth about what happens when we die?

Second, *we have no basis to believe the words of Jesus.* He
states in verse 2, "In my Father's house are many rooms; if
it were not so, I would have told you. I am going there to
prepare a place for you." If there is no heaven, there is no
Father's house—and no rooms for us!

The fact is, if there is no heaven, Jesus Christ has not
told us the truth—either because He did not intend to
(He purposely deceived us) or He did not know (He was
somehow deluded into believing in a heaven which does
not exist). Would you want to commit your life into the
hands of someone who was either deceived or is a de-
ceiver? If there is no heaven, it is a logical inference that
Jesus Christ is not Lord, but is a liar or a lunatic.

Third, if we imagine that there is no heaven, it is reasonable to conclude from John 14 that *we should have no confi-*

dence that Christ is coming back. Jesus states in verse 3, "And if I go and prepare a place for you, I will come back and take you to be with me that you also may be where I am." Christians have invested many hours studying about the Second Coming, written scores of books about it (some of which presumptuously attempt to predict the timing of that event) and held numerous Bible conferences seeking to convince one another of the specific circumstances of His return. If there is no heaven, these activities have all been *in vain!* If there is no heaven, then Jesus patently lied to us about going there to prepare a place for us, for there is no "there" there! If there is no heaven, then Jesus was going nowhere, preparing no place—and will not be coming back.

All of His parables about being faithful with our talents (Matthew 25:14-30), anticipating the owner of the house's return (Luke 12:35-48), or being busy in His work (Luke 19:11-27) mean nothing! No one's coming back. The assurance of His return which has encouraged believers for two millennia is a false assurance.

Wanna Bet?

But there are Christians who say, "Suppose we discover that there is no heaven after all? At least we have lived the best life here! We should have no regrets, for we have invested our lives in the things that really matter, even if there is no afterlife."

This argument has been classically stated by seventeenth-century French mathematician and theologian Blaise Pascal and is commonly referred to as "Pascal's Wager." Pascal argues that we are unable either to prove or disprove the existence of God and therefore we are faced with a choice. Either God exists or He doesn't. We must flip a coin in this game of life. "If you gain [by betting on God's existence], you gain all; if you lose, you lose nothing,"[8] says Pascal. And you cannot sit out of this game; you are obliged to play. The risk you take is the loss of nothingness. Pascal writes, ". . . it is certain that we risk, and that the infinite distance between the *certainty* of what is staked and the *uncertainty* of what will be gained, equals the finite good which is certainly staked against the uncertain infinite."[9] Clear? What Pascal is really arguing is that we should wager our finite lives for the gamble of an infinite life with God, and if He does not exist, we have only forfeited something finite. If, however, He does exist, we have gained the infinite!

But what of proofs, of evidences for the Christian faith, you might ask? Pascal challenges us:

> Endeavor, then, to convince yourself, not by increase of proofs of God, but by the abatement of your passions. . . . Learn of those who have been bound like you, and who now stake all their possessions. . . . Follow the way by which they began; by acting as if they believed, taking the holy water, having masses said, etc. . . . What have you to lose? . . . it is this which will lessen the passions, which are your stumbling-blocks.[10]

In the final analysis, Pascal says, a gamble on God is a win-win situation. He writes,

> Now, what harm will befall you in taking this side? You will be faithful, humble, grateful, generous, a sincere friend, truthful. Certainly you will not have those poisonous pleasures, glory and luxury; but will you not have others? I will tell you that

you will thereby gain in this life, and that, at each
step you take on this road, you will see so great
certainty of gain, so much nothingness in what
you risk, that you will at last recognize that you
have wagered for something certain and infinite,
for which you have given nothing.[11]

But if there is no heaven, it is unlikely that there is a
God—a transcendent one, at any rate. Does Pascal's wager
make sense if we "imagine there's no heaven"?

Not a "Blind Gamble"

As much as I admire Pascal for his absolute commitment
to spiritual things and for his brilliant mathematical mind, I
believe the better advice comes from Jesus, Luke and the
Apostle Paul. Jesus endorses and commends the sifting of evidence to determine if faith in Him is well-grounded. He
states in Matthew 16 that the Jewish leaders exercise their
reason when it comes to the weather (if the sky is red and
threatening, they call off their synagogue picnic). Should
they not do the same when it comes to the more important
matter of "the signs of the times" (16:1-4)?

Dr. Luke, the human author of the third gospel and of
the Acts of the Apostles, emphasizes that Jesus "showed
himself to [the apostles] and gave many convincing proofs
that he was alive" (Acts 1:3). Belief in Christ was hardly a
blind gamble for him. It was the only reasonable response
to credible and persuasive evidence.

The Apostle Paul argues in First Corinthians that "If
only for this life we have hope in Christ, we are to be pitied
more than all men. . . . If the dead are not raised, 'Let us eat
and drink, for tomorrow we die' " (15:19, 32). Paul's case

for Christianity's truthfulness in this chapter rests solely on the literal resurrection of Christ. If He has not risen from the dead, then certain conclusions are unavoidable: the preaching of the apostles is useless, as is the Christian faith of the Corinthians (15:14); the apostles deserve to be stoned to death as false witnesses for preaching the resurrection of Christ, if in fact He did not rise (15:15); belief in Christ is futile and does not rescue one from the penalty of his sins (15:17); and those loved ones who have died in Christ died believing in a false Savior (15:18).

Paul's final conclusion is that "if only for this life we have hope in Christ, we are to be pitied more than all men" (15:19). Should the Christian persevere in believing in Christ, even if the evidence indicates that He is still in the grave somewhere in Palestine? Not according to Paul! He argues that being persecuted for a false Messiah is not laudable; it is lamentable. It is not a cause for praise but an occasion for pity. In fact, Paul counsels a live-for-today philosophy if Christianity is not true: "Let us eat and drink, for tomorrow we die" (15:32).

So Paul defends the validity of Christianity by one specific event, the resurrection of Christ. The evidences for that event (note the eyewitnesses listed in 15:5-9) should drive the honest inquirer to an eyes-open faith commitment to Christ. Rather than being a flip-of-the-coin kind of decision, the resurrection of Jesus Christ supplies the believer with a solid foundation for faith. Instead of being the gamble of a gullible soul, that event rests upon historical validation which is testable. If the resurrection did not really happen, then the liberal Anglican Bishop David Jenkins is correct in dismissing Christ's resurrection as a "conjuring trick with bones."[12]

I have a great regard for how the Lord has used Dr. Billy Graham in the communication of the gospel over his fruitful life. However, I wish that he had not named his magazine "Decision" magazine for the simple reason that conversions in the book of Acts are more of the nature of *persuasions* than decisions. The evidence for Christ being the Messiah and having risen from the dead is presented by the Apostles and some people are persuaded. Of course there is a decision to make, but it is the most reasonable one which takes into account the facts.

It must be admitted, however, that there is a certain cogency in Pascal's argument for a "wager." Technically speaking, all of life involves probability—even in a "pure" science such as mathematics. We look at evidence, make reasonable inferences from the evidence, then come to certain conclusions about how to proceed further. Some scientific matters can be empirically verified or falsified by the repetition of experiments, but most of life can't be squeezed into a test tube or duplicated under laboratory conditions. That life is a kind of wager makes sense. To paraphrase the great "theologian" Bob Dylan, "You gotta believe *somebody!*"

But Pascal—along with the rest of us—needs to show that wagering one's finite life on *Christ* is the most reasonable decision. Why Him? Why Christianity? This is where the arguments from the Lord Jesus, Dr. Luke and the Apostle Paul fit in.

Historian Paul Johnson says, "Christianity, like the Judaism from which it sprang, is a historical religion, or it is nothing. It does not deal in myths and metaphors and symbols, or in states of being and cycles. It deals in facts."[13] As someone has aptly stated, "Every man is entitled to be wrong in his opinions, but no man is entitled to be wrong in his *facts!*"

Gambling with a Nightmare

So on what basis should one "imagine there's no heaven"? The fact that some people, including some Christians, are not "livin' for today"? The reality that the world is not living as one? Those realities give even *more* reason for people to consider genuine Christianity.

Lennon's dream of imagining there's no heaven is, in fact, a *nightmare*. Jesus Christ conquered death and validated His claim to be the Son of God (Romans 1:4). If He is indeed God-become-man, then His testimony of the next life for all who believe should not be questioned, but should be embraced and enjoyed!

Reasons to Believe

Rather than drawing those three depressing conclusions from Jesus' words in John 14, we can be assured that their opposites are actually the case:

First, because heaven is real, *we have every reason to trust God*. Our hearts do not have to be held hostage by worry or anxiety. God has proved Himself thoroughly trustworthy by His acts in human history. He has kept His promises, He has blessed and often forgiven His people, and He has warned the world of unbelief. Those who refuse to trust in God are not rejecting the petty demands of an irrational, self-centered potentate, but are putting themselves out of touch with the very source of Reality itself! Not trusting God means turning one's back on what life was meant to be.

Second, *we have the best reason to believe the words of Jesus*. He *has* told us the truth. He *has* gone to the Father's house to prepare a place for us. He who spent thirty years as a carpenter on earth has, in a sense, taken up that vocation again in heaven. The Father's house is a real locality to which Jesus has gone, and He is not idle there. As a bridegroom, He is getting that new home ready for the Church, His bride. He is the architect, inspector, and construction supervisor all in one.

In John 14:1 Jesus affirms, in the strongest terms possible, His own deity: "Trust in God; trust also in me." Those seven words in English are really eight words in Greek, and can be translated various ways:

"You already believe in God; now believe in Me!" or,

"You already believe in God; and you, therefore, are already believing in Me." or,

"Believe in God! And you will be believing in Me!" or,

"Believe in God! And believe in Me!"[14]

Whether those eight Greek words are to be understood as an affirmation followed by a command, two affirmations, a command followed by an affirmation or two commands cannot be determined from the passage. But no matter how one translates this verse, Jesus is making it crystal clear that He demands the same faith in Himself that the disciples already had or should have had in God! Jesus is claiming equality with the Father. He was either right or wrong, and we either believe Him or we don't.

Third, *we are not fools for looking with anticipation for His Second Coming*. His Second Coming is as reliable an event as was His first coming which culminated in His magnificent victory over death.

The story is told of a very nervous bride at her wedding rehearsal. She was fearful that she would forget where to go, when to say her vows, and everything. The minister offered help: "Honey, listen. Remember what I'm going to tell you. First, you'll walk down the *aisle*. Then you will stop next to your groom at the *altar*. Then after the *hymn*, the two of you will ascend to the platform to repeat your vows after me. Just keep in mind those three key words."

When the marriage ceremony began, all in the congregation could hear the confident bride as she strolled to the front of the church: "*I'll alter him! . . . I'll alter him! . . . I'll . . .*"

And this is Christ's stated purpose in returning to earth: to whisk away His bride to that heavenly home, after He has done the work of alteration. Don't miss this truth: He wants us with Him. We matter to Christ. He will keep His word and return for His people. We will not be left standing at the altar.

Wait-Watchers

When I was younger, I used to have an attitude about anybody who was overweight. It was easy for me to have an attitude back then, because I couldn't seem to add an ounce to my 137 pounds. Then I turned thirty-five, and the good Lord said, "Let there be a metabolic change in this arrogant, skinny person!" And lo, it came to pass. I began to notice that I was gaining weight, and gravity noticed too, seeking to drag me down into despair. Since then I've become much more understanding of those (of us) who struggle with a few (my wife would say, "what do you mean, 'a few'?") extra pounds. I've learned some new technical terms as a theologian, such as "Slim•Fast" and "Weight Watchers."

Have you ever considered the fact that every believer is to be a "*Wait*-Watcher"? We are to busy ourselves with the bridegroom's business, while we anticipate His return for us. Jesus Christ has not lied to us, nor was He deluded in His understanding of that other world. He told us the truth and is eagerly anticipating the fetching of His bride.

The Farthest Thing
from "Christmas in Heaven"

So what are we to make of John Lennon and his advice? His life of mocking Christ and his death (presumably without a saving knowledge of Christ) are, indeed, tragedies. Rather than becoming "part of God" upon his death, if he died without a personal relationship with Jesus Christ, he died "in [his] sins" (John 8:24), the worst fate possible for a human being. Instead of dying as the world's most respected martyr, he died a fool if he did not believe the gospel. Though at one time the Beatles *were* undoubtedly "more popular than Jesus," there will come a day when every knee will bow to Jesus as judge.

Paul McCartney duplicated Lennon's massive error when he suggested that John was right "in the long term." Jesus and Jesus alone knows the "long term," and when individuals die, they do not become part of God. They do not merge with the Being of the universe. They stand before the Lord and must give an account of what they have done with, what they have believed about, the Son of God. No amount of fan adoration will change one's eternal destiny after death, no matter how popular or famous one happens to have been in this life.

Imagine there's no heaven? What a foolish application of our God-given minds. Rather we should meditate on the truth revealed to us by the God who, on one occasion, hijacked one of His servants to that glorious place, as we will see in our next chapter.

TWO

Hijacked to Paradise

If I have any beliefs about immortality, it is that certain dogs I have known will go to heaven, and very, very few persons.

(James Thurber)

There was a time when you asked questions because you wanted answers, and were glad when you had found them. Become that child again: even now.

(C.S. Lewis)

I know a man in Christ who . . . was caught up to the third heaven . . . to paradise. He heard inexpressible things, things that man is not permitted to tell.

(2 Corinthians 12:2-4)

A new arrival was being shown around heaven by the Lord. "This is so wonderful," he said. "I never knew it was so great. The music is magnificent, the love is fantastic, the beauty is overwhelming. As a matter of fact, if I had known how great this really is, I would have come here sooner."

The Lord smiled and said, "Well, you could have come here sooner if you hadn't eaten so much oat bran."

As we think about getting ready for the real heaven, wouldn't it be incredible to actually go there and take a brief tour? That desire is granted not to the living, but to the dead (specifically, the damned) in C.S. Lewis' work *The Great Divorce*.[1] It is the story of a busload of hell's residents who are granted a one-day excursion to heaven to see if they would like to change locations. Rather than being a study of the afterlife, Lewis' work deals with the many reasons why people don't want to believe the gospel. Lewis' portrayal of heaven and hell is quite insightful, however.

A masterpiece of metaphor, *The Great Divorce* presents hell as "the grey town" and heaven as a place where its residents are "solid people" who seek to show the visitors why they should relocate. The visitors, however, are not solid and find the terrain of heaven painful (they can hardly walk on heaven's grass, for it does not bend under their rather unsubstantial feet). More importantly, with only one exception, all the visitors turn down the opportunity to move from hell to heaven, for they find that heaven just would not suit them. The theme of the book is clear:

> There are only two kinds of people in the end: those who say to God, "Thy will be done," and those to whom God says, in the end, "*Thy* will be done." All that are in Hell, choose it. Without that self-choice there could be no Hell. No soul that seriously and

constantly desires joy will ever miss it. Those who seek find. To those who knock it is opened.[2]

Reasons to Remain

We learn why the condemned in *The Great Divorce* refuse heaven. One man cannot bear the idea of God's mercy; he would prefer, as a "decent man," to "do it on his own." Another cannot tolerate the idea that his religious views would be penalized, that his intellectual opinions (he calls them "honest and heroic") would be rejected as false. He recoils from the concept of an environment in which truth has taken the place of "free inquiry" and forgiveness the place of "usefulness." He demands the freedom to be thirsty, even when there is life-giving water. And he cuts short his dialogue with the Holy Ghost because he has a paper to read on such crucial matters at a little Theological Society meeting back in hell.

Another rejects heaven because he is convinced it must be a conspiracy to trick him. After all, he reasons, if God were real, He would storm hell, utilizing "a more militant charity" to put it out of existence. Another substitutes his art for heaven's reality, loving his paint more than the Light.

A mother refuses heaven because she would not be promised charge over her son whom she dominated on earth. "I must have someone to—to do things to," she says. Another turns away because of his conviction that the final loss of one soul should invalidate the joy of those who are saved. This effort at blackmailing the universe—of allowing hell to veto heaven—is repudiated by heaven's citizens.

A Biblical Parable

This brings to mind the story Jesus tells in Luke 16:19-31 of two men who die on the same day.[3] One is Lazarus, a beggar who knew the Lord and is escorted by the angels into the presence of God ("Abraham's side"). The other is a rich man who lived his life without a concern for his soul and finds himself in a terrible place of punishment (Hades). The rich man sees the beggar enjoying the glories of heaven and requests that Abraham send Lazarus down to hell to comfort him in his thirst. He also asks that Lazarus be sent back to earth to warn his five living brothers not to come "to this place of torment" (16:28).

Abraham responds to the first request by referring to a "great chasm" separating those in heaven from those in hell. "Those who want to go from here to you cannot, nor can anyone cross over from there to us" (16:26), Abraham informs him. Apparently, even if Lazarus wanted to help the rich man in hell, it isn't allowed. No short-term missions trips will be sent to that far country! Nor can any of Hades' residents cross over from hell to heaven.

To the second request (that Lazarus go back to earth to warn the man's five brothers about hell), Abraham states, in effect, "Your *five* brothers have the *five* books of Moses. Let them listen to them. If they do not heed Moses and the Prophets, they will not be convinced even if someone rises from the dead" (16:29-31, author paraphrase).

I have an old King James Bible that has as the paragraph heading for Luke 16:19-31 these words: "A Soul Repents in Hell." *Nothing could be further from the truth!* The rich man is not showing repentance in hell; he is engaging in *recrimination*. He is saying, "I was not sufficiently warned about this awful place, and *my brothers* have not been sufficiently warned either. And it's *God's* fault!"

We cannot be certain, by the way, that this story of Lazarus and the rich man is a parable and not a factual account. It is the only one of Jesus' stories that contains a proper name (Lazarus), which gives a flavor more of fact than fiction. Luke also does not refer to it as a parable—but then, Luke does not use the word "parable" to introduce the story of the good Samaritan (10:30-37), the mustard seed (13:18-19), the great banquet (14:15-24), or the shrewd manager (16:1-8), either. Since the story of the rich man and Lazarus follows the story of the shrewd manager, it could be a parable. One thing is certain, however: Jesus would not mislead His followers about the nature of the afterlife (for either the lost or the saved), even in the context of a parable.

This point seems to be lost on Canadian theologian Clark Pinnock, who has attacked the doctrine of man's immortal soul. He writes in his *Theological Crossfire: An Evangelical/Liberal Dialogue*, "What is life like beyond the barrier? Christians often say that we go to heaven when we die, but this is not really an accurate way of speaking biblically."[4] Obviously, he needs to take Luke 16 more seriously. We will further examine the issue of man's immortal soul in Chapter 6.

From Lewis' fanciful bus tour of heaven to Jesus' parable about Lazarus and the rich man, we might ask the question as to whether any of the *redeemed* have ever visited heaven—and returned to tell about it. We have the story of the "other Lazarus" in John 11, a beloved friend of Jesus who dies and is brought back to life by the Lord. If our understanding of what happens when a believer dies is correct, that is, that his soul or spirit immediately goes to be with the Lord at death, then it is reasonable to assume that this other Lazarus had been in heaven with the Lord. When the Lord Jesus raises his body in John 11, we presume that Lazarus' spirit was reunited with his body on earth. But we are given no details as to what Lazarus experienced during those several days that his soul or spirit was separated from his body.

There are several books on the market which claim to be eyewitness accounts of a vision of—or a trip to—heaven. We will look indepth at one of these claims in our fourth chapter. But do we have any authoritative *biblical* accounts of such a visit to glory? The answer is yes!

A Holy Hijacking

The Apostle Paul describes someone who had just such an experience in Second Corinthians 12. Let's look at the first six verses:

> I must go on boasting. Although there is nothing to be gained, I will go on to visions and revelations from the Lord. I know a man in Christ who fourteen years ago was caught up to the third heaven. Whether it was in the body or out of the body I do not know—God knows. And I know that this man—whether in the body or apart from the body I do not know, but God knows—was caught up to paradise. He heard inexpressible things, things that man is not permitted to tell. I will boast about a man like that, but I will not boast about myself, except about my weaknesses. Even if I should choose to boast, I would not be a fool, because I would be speaking the truth. But I refrain, so no one will think more of me than is warranted by what I do or say.

Several things are notable about this account of being "hijacked to paradise."[5] The first is the context of this event. In the previous chapter in Second Corinthians, Paul has resorted to the absurd practice of boasting in order to defend his apostleship and show that he is not inferior to those so-called "super-apostles" (11:5) who are really "false apostles" (11:13; cf. Galatians 1:8). Paul brags about his sufferings for the sake of the gospel (2 Corinthians 11:16-29) and concludes his laundry list of persecutions by stating, "If I must boast, I will boast of the things that show my weakness" (11:30). It is at this point that Paul talks about this man who was "caught up to paradise" (12:4).

A Brief English Review

One unusual feature of Paul's account in Second Corinthians 12 is his use of the third person: "I know *a man*," Paul says (12:2). "*This man* . . . was caught up to paradise. . . . He heard inexpressible things, things that man is not permitted to tell" (12:3-4). Paul appears to be describing the experience of someone other than himself. He even draws a distinction between himself and this person in verse 5 ("I will boast about a man like that, but I will not boast about myself, except about my weaknesses"). Why would Paul boast about something that happened to someone else?

Let us clearly establish that he is, indeed, describing his own, rather than someone else's, experience. How would an experience such as being "caught up to the third heaven" fit into Paul's "boasting" about *his* apostleship if the experience happened to someone else? But if he *is* talking about himself, why does he use the third person?

It becomes clear that he is speaking about himself when he shifts to the *first* person in verse 6: "Even if I should choose to boast, I would not be a fool, because I would be speaking the truth. But I refrain, so no one will think more of me than is warranted by what I do or say." Paul is hinting here that he could have described this experience in the first person ("This happened to *me!*"), but he is afraid that such boasting would be going too far. His humility forces him to write about it as if it happened to someone else.

He really lets the cat out of the bag in verses 7-10:

> To keep me from becoming conceited because of these surpassingly great revelations, there was given me a thorn in my flesh, a messenger of Satan, to torment me. Three times I pleaded with the Lord to take it away from me. But he said to me, "My grace is sufficient for you, for my power is made perfect in weakness." Therefore I will boast all the more gladly about my weaknesses, so that Christ's power may rest on me. That is why, for Christ's sake, I delight in weaknesses, in insults, in hardships, in persecutions, in difficulties. For when I am weak, then I am strong.

Note Paul's shift to the *first* person—he uses it *thirteen times* to indicate that being "caught up to paradise" happened to *him*. The reward for this magnificent experience? A thorn in the flesh, a messenger of Satan, is given to keep him from becoming conceited about these "surpassingly great revelations" (12:7). What sense would it make for Paul to get such a gift for someone else's experience? And how exactly does one become conceited about a revelation that another has had? This is Paul's unobtrusive way of admitting that *he* was the man "caught up to paradise."

Why the Late News Report?

Having established that it was none other than the Apostle Paul who had this experience, several questions must be discussed. Why did Paul wait *fourteen years* to talk about this major event (12:2)? Today an individual would go on a speaking tour, make a video, develop a web site, conduct a seminar—at least write a book about such a revelation! Why would Paul stay quiet about this for over a dozen years?

Paul does not explain his silence to us. What he does do is pull out this experience like a trump card in defending his apostleship. It is as if he is saying, "You think those so-called 'super-apostles' have credibility? Something to boast about? How about a personal tour of heaven? And you know what I got for it? A messenger from Satan, a thorn in my flesh that God refuses to remove!" In the absurd context of a kind of apostolic can-you-top-this, Paul concludes that his only appropriate boast should be in his weakness.

Details, Please!

But what are the details of this experience of the apostle? Note that he says two times that he doesn't know whether this being "caught up to paradise" happened "in the body or apart from the body" (12:3-4). What does he mean by those expressions? Similar language is used by Paul in Second Corinthians 5:6-9:

> Therefore we are always confident and know that as long as we are *at home in the body* we are *away from the Lord*. We live by faith, not by sight. We are confident, I say, and would prefer to be away from the body and at home with the Lord. So we make it our goal to please him, whether we are *at home in the body* or *away from it*.

In this text Paul presents us with a simple either-or situation. If a person is "at home in the body," then that person is somehow "away from the Lord." Paul's preference would be to "be away from the body" and consequently to be "at home with the Lord." Whatever his condition, Paul's ultimate concern is to please the Lord, "whether we are at home in the body or away from it." The reference seems to be to *life* or *death*. When we are alive in this world ("in the body"), we are separated from the Lord. When we have died in this world ("away from the body"), we will then be "at home with the Lord." Paul does not envision a third state which some today suggest, namely "soul-sleep," a doctrine that the believer "sleeps" in the grave in an unconscious condition until the resurrection.

In Philippians Paul also uses similar language:

> I eagerly expect and hope that I will in no way be ashamed, but will have sufficient courage so that now as always Christ will be exalted in my body, whether by life or by death. For to me, to live is Christ and to die is gain. If I am to go on living in the body, this will mean fruitful labor for me. Yet what shall I choose? I do not know! I am torn between the two: I desire to depart and be with Christ, which is better by far; but it is more necessary for you that I remain in the body. Convinced of this, I know that I will remain, and I will continue with all of you for your progress and joy in the faith, so that through my being with you again your joy in Christ Jesus will overflow on account of me. (1:20-26)

There is no question in this Philippians passage that Paul is speaking of two states of existence: life or death. He wishes that he could depart his body and be with Christ. Again, there is no indication of a third state of being, of something between life in the body and one's presence with the Lord (out of one's earthly body).

So what are we to make of Paul's "in the body or out of the body" language in Second Corinthians 12? He may be saying that he does not know whether he was taken bodily to heaven or became temporarily separated from his earthly body (i.e., *dead!*). What he *does* know is that his experience was real and had profound implications for his own life. At any rate, the idea of the soul or spirit being temporarily separated from the body (apart from physical death) does not appear to be taught in the Bible.

So what was it that Paul experienced? He uses several cryptic expressions which we need to examine. He speaks of "visions and revelations from the Lord" (12:1), of being "caught up to the third heaven" (12:2), of being "caught up to paradise" (12:4), of having "heard inexpressible things, things that man is not permitted to tell" (12:4) and of having received "surpassingly great revelations" (12:7). These terms indicate sensory experience (specifically auditory and visual) of the reality of heaven!

Jewish tradition tells us of four rabbis who had this kind of vision of God. Ben Azai saw God's glory and died from the experience. Ben Soma went mad as a result of his vision. Acher, another rabbi, is said to have "cut up the young plants," meaning that he became a heretic as a result of the vision, ruining the garden of truth. Akiba is the fourth rabbi and we are told that he ascended in peace and in peace came back.[6] What results did this experience have on the Apostle Paul? Let's notice what he tells us.

A Sanctioned Silence

Paul "heard inexpressible things, things that man is not permitted to tell" (12:4). What will we *hear* when we get to heaven? We know that we will hear the praises of the angels, especially the cherubim who cry out day and night before the Lord, "Holy, holy, holy is the Lord God Almighty, who was, and is, and is to come" (Revelation 4:8). One is reminded of C.S. Lewis' words in *The Great Divorce*: "If I could remember their singing and write down the notes, no man who read that score would ever grow sick or old."[7] He also defines heaven as "the regions where there is only life and therefore all that is not music is silence."[8]

The expression "inexpressible things" comes from a Greek adjective which either refers to something that *cannot* be expressed, since it is beyond human powers, or to something that *must not* be expressed, since it is holy.[9] Used here in Second Corinthians 12, the term seems to imply both meanings: what Paul heard is beyond the capacity of human language to describe and he is forbidden from trying, for he says he heard "things that man is not permitted to tell" (or, it is not proper to speak of). His trip to heaven brought him into a context where the things he heard drove him to silence because of the paucity of human language and the absence of divine permission. Being left *speechless* by the sounds of heaven, he can only describe them as "inexpressible." You cannot apply that word to too many things today, but heaven certainly fits that category!

A Visual Spectacle

Paul not only *heard* inexpressible things which man is not permitted to tell, he also had "visions and revelations from the Lord" (12:1). He describes himself as one who was "caught up to the third heaven" (12:2), and as one who was "caught up to paradise" (12:4). This verb used in both these sentences means to steal, carry off, drag away or snatch.[10] It is the same word used to describe one who is "snatch[ed] . . . from the fire" in Jude 23 and also to describe the Apostle Philip in Acts 8:39, where we read, "the Spirit of the Lord suddenly took Philip away."

The implication seems to be that Paul did not seek this experience; it happened without his pursuit or permission. The expressions "third heaven" and "paradise" appear to be equivalent terms, for Paul is speaking about the same experience. The term "paradise" is also used in Luke 23:43 regarding Jesus' promise to the repentant thief on the cross: "I tell you the truth, today you will be with me in *paradise*." We also read in Revelation 2:7 about the "tree of life, which is in the *paradise* of God."

There are some who argue that "paradise" is not the same as heaven, but was rather a "holding tank" for Old Testament believers who awaited the atoning work of Christ, before they could be ushered into heaven itself by a resurrected Savior. However, the evidence for this position is lacking in the total witness of the Scriptures, and appears to be more of a Catholic (and later, dispensational) belief in a compartmentalized place of the dead.

What did Paul experience *visually*? He uses the rather cryptic expression "visions and revelations from the Lord" (2 Corinthians 12:1), and refers in verse 7 to "these surpassingly great revelations." He does not tell us what he saw. The term "visions" refers to one being granted the privilege by God of seeing what is ordinarily hidden from human beings (this same word is used by Paul when he describes his vision on the road to Damascus in Acts 26).[11] The term "revelation" implies the disclosing or revealing of some truth or information. As one scholar explains it,

"In Second Corinthians 12:1 Paul is connecting both words in the one prepositional phrase . . . and saying that he was permitted to see something usually hidden from men and in the seeing, some basic divine truth was made known to him, a revelation from the Lord."[12] Heaven is usually hidden from human eyes, but Paul gets a front-row seat. Beyond these descriptions Paul does not go.

These few tantalizing details are all we have of Paul's hijacking to paradise. He does not refer to this event anywhere else in his writings; in fact, he only brings up the experience here to contrast boasting in the flesh with boasting in one's weakness.

Paul's reticence to speak of his trip to heaven should give pause to any who claim a similar experience. But the enticements to go into detail are hard to resist. We will examine one contemporary claim of a visit to heaven in our next chapter.

A Hijacking with a Purpose

So what do we learn about heaven from our considerations in this chapter? We learn that heaven is a real place awaiting the Christian (it was real enough that the Apostle Paul needed a thorn in his flesh to keep him from becoming conceited about its reality). We learn that words and word pictures are insufficient to describe it. Efforts to "put heaven into words" ought not to go beyond the Bible, for they *caricature* heaven rather than communicate it. We also learn that heaven *awaits* the believer and is worth waiting for! We learn that Paul brings up this event not in order to give details about that next life, but to give encouragement about living for Christ in *this* life.

In our next chapter we will notice three individuals who held wrong thoughts of heaven. As we examine their viewpoints we will gain further perspective on how we are to live in this world as we get ready for that next world.

THREE

Wrong Thoughts of Heaven

"Almost heaven—West Virginia . . ."

(John Denver)

"If the Bible is true, then I'm Christ."

(David Koresh)

"I was wrong."

(Jim Bakker)

"If my kingdom were of this world, then would my servants fight."

(Jesus in John 18:36, KJV)

O n Sunday, October 12, 1997, Henry John Deutschendorf Jr. was enjoying Monterey Bay, California, from a unique perspective. He was several thousand feet above that scenic area in his experimental aircraft. The only problem, according to news reports, was that Mr. Deutschendorf apparently did not know how to engage the emergency fuel tank, and his craft ran out of gas, plunging him to his death.

Better known as John Denver, this world-renowned artist had two passions: flying and outer space. As a licensed
pilot with his own Lear jet, Denver also engaged in aero-
batics and enjoyed gliders.

Although he flew F-15 fighters and even spent time in the
Space Shuttle simulator, Denver's real career was his music.
He had fourteen gold and eight platinum albums in the U.S.
alone. His popularity at home and overseas earned him a
place as one of the top five recording artists in the history of
the music industry. His 1973 album, "John Denver's
Greatest Hits," remains one of the biggest sellers in the history of RCA Records, with over 10 million copies distributed
worldwide.

Once asked by the senior music editor of *Reader's Digest*
how he would like to ultimately be remembered, Denver
said,

> I think what people are going to remember about
> me are my songs. I have worked really hard to find
> out who I am. I've had the courage to do what I
> think is right: to be true to myself and write the
> things that come out of me. That is how I hope my
> children remember me.[1]

Denver's two divorces and two drunken-driving arrests
were a sort of epiphany, friends at his funeral said. He was
writing a new song that he hoped would have commercial
potential.

A World in Balance?

His songwriting skills were first noticed when Peter, Paul,
and Mary recorded his "Leaving on a Jet Plane," a song
which became their first number one hit. Denver followed

with hits of his own: "Take Me Home, Country Roads,"
"Rocky Mountain High," "Sunshine On My Shoulders,"
"Annie's Song," "Back Home Again," and "Thank God I'm
a Country Boy." Many of his songs focused on environmental concerns. He once stated: "I want to work in whatever I
do—my music, my writing, my performing, my commit-
ments, my home and personal life—in a way that is directed
towards a world in balance, a world that creates a better
quality of life for all people."[2] Critics mocked Denver's syrupy
tunes on occasion. He responded, "I want people to feel the
goodness in their own lives."[3]

He co-founded the Windstar Foundation, a nonprofit
environmental education and research center in 1976
that works toward a sustainable future for the world. He
once enumerated "the things which are so important to
me: the environment and the sense of global community
which we're moving closer and closer to, whether we recognize it or not."[4]

His humanitarian efforts included a tour of the Soviet Union in 1985 and a benefit concert for the victims of
Chernobyl in 1987. As a member of the Presidential Commission on World and Domestic Hunger, he was also one of
the five founders of The Hunger Project. Awarded the Presidential "World without Hunger" Award, he was also a sup-
porter of the National Wildlife Federation, Save the
Children, the Cousteau Society, Friends of the Earth and the
Human/Dolphin Foundation, to name just a few. Before his
death he created "Plant-It 2000," a re-forestation project
which led to the planting of nearly 100,000 trees in its first
year of operation.

Among many other honors, in 1993 he became the first
non-classical music artist to receive the prestigious Albert

Schweitzer Music Award, "for a life's work dedicated to music and devoted to humanity."

One line in Denver's song, "Take Me Home, Country Roads," explains his connection with the subject of this book: "Almost heaven—West Virginia . . ." There is no doubt that the beauty of the West Virginian mountains seems celestial, but the best this world has to offer is but a faint reflection of that eternal home for the believer.

As much as we might respect the ecological concerns of the late performer, Denver's life seemed to show more concern for this world than for the next. Was he prepared to meet his Maker when he plummeted to earth? More specifically, what had he done with Jesus Christ in this world, a world which, because of sin, is anything but "a world in balance"? Rather than feeling the "goodness" of his own life, did he recognize his own *sin*—and need of a Savior? Had he filled his own soul with the only Bread which could satisfy his spiritual hunger—Jesus Christ? If he had, he kept it a secret, because there seems to be no evidence that John Denver was prepared for that heavenly environment. West Virginia could be the only "heaven" he will ever experience.

Apocalypse Now!

Vernon Howell was raised in a mainstream Seventh-Day Adventist Church, dropping out of school in the ninth grade. In 1990 Howell changed his name to Koresh, Hebrew for Cyrus, the Persian king who allowed the Jews to return to Israel after their Babylonian captivity. David Koresh became the leader of the Branch Davidians outside Waco, Texas, as a result of an armed conflict with a Benjamin Roden (now in a mental hospital), a preacher who described himself as the literal successor to King David of Israel.

Koresh's apocalyptic theology merged with a kind of secular survivalism. His 100 followers began to stockpile food and weapons in their compound, which was the size of a city block. Federal agents tracked shipments to the group, estimating that almost four tons of ammunition and enough parts to assemble hundreds of automatic and semiautomatic weapons were accumulated by the Davidians. One carton split open before it could be delivered by the United Parcel Service. It contained hand grenades.[5]

Koresh's theology was quite simple. He said, "If the Bible is true, then I'm Christ." And he believed that he had been sent down to earth to be a sinful Jesus so that, when he stood in judgment of sinners on Judgment Day, he would have experience of all sin and degradation. That degradation included ruling his followers with an iron fist, exercising corporal punishment on the children, separating the men from their wives, and having sexual relations with the female members of his commune. Some of his "wives" were perhaps as young as eleven or twelve.

This "mad messiah of Waco" entertained a vision of martyrdom for himself, teaching that he would die in a battle against unbelievers. He would be joined in heaven by those followers who had laid down their lives in armed conflict for him. One hardly needs to point out that Koresh missed the real Jesus' clear declaration that "If my kingdom were of this world, then would my servants fight" (John 18:36, KJV).

In 1993 when day fifty-one of the federal government siege of the Branch Davidian compound came, fire destroyed dozens of people, including David Koresh. Some suggest that the Oklahoma City bombing of the Alfred P.

Murrah Federal Building two years later, which took the lives of 168 men, women and children, was done by Timothy McVeigh and Terry Nichols in retaliation for the attack on Waco.

From all available evidence, it appears that Koresh was either deeply disturbed or incredibly evil—or both. And if he met his death without being "in Christ," that is, without a saving relationship with the real Messiah, then, according to the Bible, he is now eternally separated from God.

On hearing it said of Francis Thompson, author of *The Hound of Heaven*, that the great tragedy of his life was that he never felt at home, a colleague of Thompson responded, "Our great tragedy is that we do!" Attempts to transform this life into heaven have failed abysmally; from the utopian efforts of the early nineteenth century to calamitous cults like the Branch Davidians and Heaven's Gate, to the contemporary "health and prosperity" movement, such attempts have either undervalued heaven or overvalued earth—or both. How foolish—and sad—to confuse the two!

The late Malcolm Muggeridge, former editor of *Punch* magazine and a latecomer to Christianity, expressed the confusing of the two worlds in one of his prayers: "Lord—The only ultimate disaster that can befall us, I have come to realize, is to feel ourselves to be at home here on earth. As long as we are aliens we cannot forget our true homeland, which is that other kingdom You proclaimed."[6]

Health and Wealth Now!

The faith movement, sometimes called the "name-it-and-claim-it" gospel, has had some very successful spokespeople push its message of a kind of heaven on earth. Jerry Savelle, one of its major figures, declares, "There is no reason for you to wait until you get to heaven to receive the blessing of God. . . . [T]he time for prosperity is now."[7] Gloria Copeland, the author of such books as *And Jesus Healed Them All, God's Will for Your Healing,* and *God's Will Is Prosperity,* comments on Mark 10:30's promise of a hundredfold return to those who have sacrificed for Christ's sake:

> Give one house and receive one hundred houses or one house worth one hundred times as much. Give one airplane and receive one hundred times the value of the airplane. Give one car and the return would furnish you a lifetime of cars. In short, Mark 10:30 is a very good deal.[8]

Gloria's husband, Kenneth Copeland, has stated that "the basic principle of the Christian life is to know that God put our sin, sickness, disease, sorrow, grief, *and poverty* on Jesus at Calvary."[9] Another leader in the movement, Robert Tilton, said that "being poor is a sin."[10] Tilton is the disgraced (and twice-divorced) evangelist who was exposed by ABC's PrimeTime Live in 1991 for taking his followers' money and throwing away their prayer requests.

Jim Bakker, imprisoned for the PTL collapse, wrote a letter to his followers when he was incarcerated, in which he acknowledged that he had been wrong about prosperity in this life being the birthright of the believer:

> Many today believe that the evidence of God's blessing on them is a new car, a house, a good job, and riches. . . . That is far from the truth of God's Word. If that be the case, then gambling casino owners and drug kingpins and movie stars are blessed of God. . . . Jesus did not teach riches were a

> sign of God's blessing. . . . I have spent months read-
> ing every word Jesus spoke. I wrote them out over
> and over, and I read them over and over again.
> There is no way, if you take the whole counsel of
> God's Word, that you can equate riches or material
> things as a sign of God's blessing.[11]

This man, whose gold plumbing fixtures, air-conditioned
doghouses, and bilking of senior citizens outraged America
and led to his being convicted of twenty-four counts of fraud
in 1989, confessed his theological error in promoting prosperity theology:

> I have asked God to forgive me and I ask all who
> have sat under my ministry to forgive me for
> preaching a gospel emphasizing earthly prosperity.
> If we equate earthly possessions and earthly rela-
> tionships with God's favor, what are we to tell the
> billions of those living in poverty? . . . It's time the
> call from the pulpit be changed from "Who wants
> the life of pleasure and good things, new homes,
> cars, material possessions, etc.?" to "Who will
> come forward to accept Jesus Christ and the fel-
> lowship of his suffering?"[12]

Bakker wrote in 1992 that "I believe the heart of God is
grieved when we cannot delay self-gratification for earthly
things in exchange for life in eternity with Him."[13]

In his book *I Was Wrong*, Bakker writes:

> As the true impact of Jesus' words regarding
> money impacted my heart and mind, I became
> physically nauseated. I was wrong. I was wrong!
> Wrong in my lifestyle, certainly, but even more

fundamentally, wrong in my understanding of the
Bible's true message. Not only was I wrong, but I
was teaching the opposite of what Jesus had said.[14]

Later, he says, "Tragically, too late, I recognized that at
PTL I had been doing just the opposite of Jesus' words, by
teaching people to fall in love with money."[15] He con-
fesses, "I had studied every word of Jesus over a period of
two years, and I was convinced that the prosperity message
was at best an aberration and at worst 'another gospel'
contrary to the gospel of Jesus Christ."[16]

Aliens and Strangers

The Apostle Peter admonishes us to "live your lives as
strangers here in reverent fear" (1 Peter 1:17). Why should
the follower of Jesus Christ live as a stranger? Peter tells us in
the next verse: "For you know that it was not with perishable
things such as silver or gold that you were redeemed from the
empty way of life handed down to you from your forefathers,
but with the precious blood of Christ, a lamb without blemish or defect" (1 Peter 1:18-19). We've been purchased *for
another world*! To live this life as if earth were heaven is to
deny our redemption by the Savior.

C.S. Lewis once remarked: "Prosperity knits a man to the
world. He feels that he is 'finding his place in it,' while really
it is finding its place in him."[17] This world is not our permanent home. Peter does not connect our stranger status only
with our redemption, however. He insists in his second
chapter that the Christian life is to be proactively lived out in
this world because of our home in *that* world:

Dear friends, I urge you, as *aliens and strangers in the
world*, to abstain from sinful desires, which war against

your soul. Live such good lives *among the pagans* that,
though they accuse you of doing wrong, they may see
your good deeds and glorify God on the day he visits
us. (1 Peter 2:11-12)

Rather than the doctrine of heaven being simply "pie in
the sky by and by," the believer's ultimate destiny should
elicit both a negative and a positive response, as Titus 2:12
points out. The negative response is that the Christian is to
get in the battle against sinful desires, "to say 'No' to ungodli-
ness and worldly passions." The positive response is that the
Christian should live such an exemplary life that the watching pagan world will have no choice but to glorify God: "to
live self-controlled, upright and godly lives in this present
age." By the way, the expression "in this present age" in Titus
2 literally reads in the Greek language: "in the *now* world."

Missing Heaven?

What do the three men discussed above have to do with
our glorious subject, heaven? The answer is, as far as we can
tell, they missed it. John Denver devoted his life to humanitarian and environmental concerns in *this* life and evidently
never gave any thought to Jesus Christ. On the other hand,
David Koresh thought he *was* the Christ! His apocalyptic
reading of the Bible and his megalomania placed him on a
fast-track to martyrdom. Perhaps only the intervention of
the law kept his martyrdom mindset from leading to the destruction of more than the several dozen who died. Given
enough time—and media coverage—his numbers might
have rivaled Jim Jones and the Guyana tragedy (900).

From the apparent position of John Denver (no after-
this-life heaven to be all that concerned about) to David

Koresh (heaven is martyrdom for his sake), we moved to Jim Bakker (heaven in this world). His ideal was not like the utopian movements of a past age, which emphasized *man's* ability to create paradise on earth. The drugged-out physician-turned-hippie Timothy Leary advised us to "Trust the evolutionary process—it will all turn out alright!"[18] The behaviorist B.F. Skinner optimistically commented in his book, *Beyond Freedom and Dignity*, "We have not yet seen what man can make of man."[19]

Bakker's confidence was not in the innate goodness of man, however, but in what he perceived to be the guarantees of God in the Bible to bring health, wealth and prosperity now. Now that he is out of prison, perhaps he can correct some of his teachings. Let's pray that he does not squander the opportunity.

The Great In-Between

We are living in the great in-between. This world is not heaven, but neither is it hell. In Hebrews 11, the great "Hall of Faith" chapter, we read of believers who by faith lived—and died—for God. The "ancients" were commended for being sure of what they hoped for and certain of what they did not see (11:1-2). Abraham obeyed God's call to leave his home, the writer of Hebrews says, "for he was looking forward to the city with foundations, whose architect and builder is God" (11:10; see also John 14:1-3). All these people (Abel, Enoch, Noah, and Abraham)

> were still living by faith when they died. They did not receive the things promised; they only saw them and welcomed them from a distance. And they admitted that they were aliens and strangers on earth.

... They were longing for a better country—a heavenly one. Therefore God is not ashamed to be called their God, for he has prepared a city for them. (Hebrews 11:13, 16)

Moses is spoken of as one who

chose to be mistreated along with the people of God rather than to enjoy the pleasures of sin for a short time. He regarded disgrace for the sake of Christ as of greater value than the treasures of Egypt, because he was looking ahead to his reward. By faith he left Egypt, not fearing the king's anger; he persevered because he saw him who is invisible. (11:25-27)

Time fails the writer of the epistle to the Hebrews, for he wishes he could discuss the victories of Gideon, Barak, Samson, Jephthah, David, Samuel and the prophets. He mentions their mighty conquests, then seamlessly moves to the enumerating of "others who were tortured and refused to be released, so that they might gain a better resurrection" (11:35). The writer lists a variety of tortures that these other members of the "Hall of Faith" endured (jeers, flogging, imprisonment, stoning, being sawed in two, and being killed by the sword). He mentions some who "went about in sheepskins and goatskins" (11:37), perhaps referring to the inhumane stadium games in which wild dogs or lions would be released to attack believers dressed up in the skins of animals.

Delay Does Not Equal Denial

Hebrews makes it clear that "these were all commended for their faith, yet none of them received what had been promised. God had planned something better for us so that only together with us would they be made perfect" (11:39-40). The failure to receive the promises of God in this life does not negate those promises. Delay does not equal denial. There is another venue where God's promises will be fulfilled and His people perfected. That other place is called *heaven*.

Implications for Christians

What are we to make of such figures as John Denver, David Koresh and Jim Bakker? Obviously, we followers of Jesus Christ are to be concerned about this world, its environment and its future. We are to be careful stewards not only of the manifold *grace* of God (1 Peter 4:10), but of the multi-dimensional *grounds* of God (Genesis 2:15). As a Bible college teacher friend of mine says, "God has given us all things richly to enjoy, not all things richly to destroy!" John Denver's life reminds us, at least to some degree, of our creation mandate to exercise careful dominion over God's world.

We need to recapture the attitude and reputation of the early followers of Christ who were praised for their concern for this world in a letter written about the year A.D. 150:

> The Christians are distinguished from other men neither by country, nor language, nor the customs which they observe. For they neither inhabit cities of their own, nor employ a peculiar form of speech, nor lead a life which is marked out by any singularity. . . . They dwell in their own countries, but simply as sojourners. As citizens, they share in all things with others, and yet endure all things as if foreigners. Every foreign land is to them as their native country, and every land of their birth as a

> land of strangers. . . . They are in the flesh, but
> they do not live after the flesh. They pass their
> days on earth, but they are citizens of heaven.
> They obey the prescribed laws, and at the same
> time surpass the laws by their lives. They love all
> men, and are persecuted by all. . . . They are poor,
> yet make many rich. . . . To sum up all in one
> word: "what the soul is in the body, that are Chris-
> tians in the world."[20]

But in exercising our dominion mandate we neither worship nature nor treat this world as our permanent home.
While all believers should care about the environment, not
all are called to focus their lifework on saving seals, preserving the wetlands, or studying the speech patterns of the
humpback whale. Some Christians are led into such careers,
but they must not allow the distinction between the animal
world and human beings made in the image and likeness of
their Creator to become blurred.[21] Nor should they honor or
esteem this world in a way which overlooks its fallen condition. As C.S. Lewis argues, we should be careful of the term
"Mother Nature." She is not our mother, he writes, but our
sister, for she too is fallen.[22]

The believer is to strive for a balance between caring for
this world over which God has given mankind stewardship
and preparing for that next world which is being readied by
the Savior (John 14:1-3). The accusation that some Christians are "so heavenly minded that they are of no earthly
good" is not a compliment! Again, it is Lewis who helps us
gain a biblical perspective on keeping one foot in each world:

> If you read history you will find that the Christians
> who did most for the present world were just those

who thought most of the next. The Apostles themselves, who set on foot the conversion of the Roman Empire, the great men who built up the Middle Ages, the English Evangelicals who abolished the Slave Trade, all left their mark on Earth, precisely because their minds were occupied with Heaven. It is since Christians have largely ceased to think of the other world that they have become so ineffective in this. Aim at Heaven and you will get earth "thrown in"; aim at earth and you will get neither.[23]

Elsewhere Lewis writes, "Because we love something else more than this world we love even this world better than those who know no other."[24]

But this world is not our home. David Koresh's sad legacy is that of a deluded fanatic who saw this world conspiring against him and his followers. Even though the Bible teaches that the Christian has three enemies—the *world*, the flesh and the devil—it does not teach that we are to declare war against this life or this world's peoples. There is no justification for God's people to set up compounds in the wilderness and begin stockpiling automatic weapons.

We *are* called to turn away from worldliness—the perspective which supplants eternal values with temporal ones, the mindset that ignores God and His Word. Christians are to be salt and light in this world as their Savior commanded (Matthew 5:13-14). We are to have a preserving impact upon the good in society (our "salt" role) and an illuminating presence upon the evil in society (our "light" role). We are to do good to all people (Galatians 6:10)—and that does not involve learning how to fire AK-47s or hurl hand grenades!

The lives of Jim and Tammy Faye Bakker stand as stark warnings of the seductive power of popularity and influence in the Christian media. Confusion about the Christian's role in society and the place of material possessions in the believer's life seems to be the moral of their unhappy story. My family and I visited Heritage Village in North Carolina where the Bakkers had invested their lives during their PTL ministry. The unfinished luxury hotel is in shambles; the amusement park is a rusted ruin. Volunteers have to come in to take care of the camels and sheep which were to be used in the passion plays.

We are not saying that God's people can't possess wealth (note the God-bestowed material blessings of Abraham, Job, etc., in the Old Testament). But the temptation to focus on the trinkets of this world is more than most Christians can bear. And like the saints enumerated in Hebrews 11, there is an inheritance laid up for the believer *in glory* which should give all Christians wisdom in living life in this world. Getting ready for that next world happens in this world. And there are many pitfalls for the child of God. As we will see in our next chapter, one of the greatest pitfalls is to claim to possess more information about eternity than God has given us in His Word.

FOUR

Heaven Only Knows!

If only God would give me some sign, like a large bank account in Switzerland.

(Woody Allen)

It is unwise for Christians to claim any knowledge of either the furniture of heaven or the temperature of hell.

(Reinhold Niebuhr)

I have made a covenant with God that he sends me neither visions, dreams, nor even angels. I am well satisfied with the gift of the Holy Scriptures which give me abundant instruction and all that I need to know both for this life and for that which is to come.

(Martin Luther)

Sanctify them by the truth; your word is truth.

(Jesus, in John 17:17)

D o you have the ability to see "MagicEye" pictures—those computer-generated patterns that, if stared at correctly, reveal a hidden picture? By looking at the pattern somewhat cross-eyedly, you may see seals balancing brightly colored balls, wolves in a desert scene, or hot-air balloons soaring in a cloudless sky, where there had only been jumbled little pieces of red, blue or brown before. For those who can't see the hidden picture, it's kind of funny to watch them try, again and again, and then say, "Oh, I see it!" But when you ask them what "it" is, they don't have a clue!

God has given me a gift which goes way beyond the "MagicEye" entertainment.[1] *I am able to look at any patterned piece of fabric, wallpaper, or even a colorful necktie, and see hidden images behind the patterns!* In fact, the image I see often directly relates to the problem or issue bothering the Christian who has come to me for biblical advice.

I had one young man come to see me, and before he could tell me what his problem was, I asked him to stand up and let me stare at his necktie. It was a silk tie, fairly expensive, and had a kind of madras look to it. I needed only a few seconds of staring intently at his tie for the image to be clearly brought out. It was a scene of an angry man and a young, crying woman who had their backs to one another.

"Having marital problems, are you?" I asked the young man.

"Yes, how did you know?"

"Well, let's say that God has given me a gift. The image I see says that the two of you are fairly close to getting divorced."

"Is there hope for reconciliation?" he asked with great emotion.

"I'm not sure," I replied. "It would help me greatly if you could bring your wife to talk with me."

"OK," he said.

I then added, "But make sure she wears a patterned dress!"

At this point, you must know I'm only joking (and if not, how gullible can you get?). And yet, many believers show little discernment in evaluating the claims of pseudo-Christian charlatans with sales pitches hardly more plausible than mine. It seems that merely *claiming* special knowledge or insight into spiritual matters (especially the doctrine of the afterlife) is all that some need to do to gain a following.

A Tour of Heaven

Wouldn't it be terrific if a Christian were caught up to heaven and wrote about it, for the benefit of all believers? Donald Brubaker's *Absent from the Body* (Peninsula Publications, 1996), Rita Bennett's *To Heaven and Back* (Zondervan, 1997), Richard E. Eby's *Caught Up into Paradise* (Revell, 1978) and others all purport to be just that—genuine accounts of those who have been to the Other Side and have come back to tell about it.

There are, of course, problems with these reports. For example, Percy Collett (who has produced a series of taped messages on his alleged celestial travels), seems obsessed with angels, suggesting that if we know where to find our "personal angel," we can "hug and kiss him." He says that there is a "Holy Ghost elevator" that takes one up to an area to observe tons of diamonds God is using to build heaven. Dogs in heaven do not bark, but horses praise God. God the Father can be seen. He is bigger than Jesus and has feathers on his left hand.[2]

One critic of Collett's claims reminds us that "Spiritists claim such [out-of-body] experiences through drugs, meditation and hypnosis. Medical explanation of this common phenomenon ranges from oxygen deficiency to the brain, chemical imbalances, hallucinations, [or] dreams to psychological illusions. The possibility of an occult experience cannot be discounted."[3] Collett actually claims that Jesus told him he would never die, but that he would go to heaven in the same manner Elijah did.[4]

The Baxter Bestsellers

Mary K. Baxter, a grandmother from Tennessee, claims to have had visions of both hell and heaven. In her two books *A Divine Revelation of Hell* and *A Divine Revelation of Heaven*[5] she states that Jesus took her on numerous trips to hell over a thirty-day period in 1976. This horrendous adventure was followed by a ten-day series of trips to heaven. Her first book sold over half a million copies and reached number five on the Christian bestseller list.

Believing that she has the gift of dreams, visions and revelations, Mrs. Baxter is convinced that Jesus chose her to proclaim the reality of hell and heaven. She claims Jesus said to her,

> For this purpose you were born, to write and tell what I have shown and told you, for these things are faithful and true. Your call is to let the world know that there is a heaven, that there is a hell, and that I, Jesus, was sent by the Father to save them from torment and to prepare them a place in heaven.[6]

She has no doubt as to her divinely appointed mission: "The book you write," Jesus tells her, "will save many souls

from hell."[7] Dr. T.L. Lowery, who writes the foreword to
Mrs. Baxter's book on heaven, says, "The inspired writings of
Mary Kathryn Baxter are divinely anointed by God. . . ."[8]
She appears to put her writing on the same plane as the Bible
when she says in one place, "Read chapters 3 and 14 of the
Gospel of John. And please read this book [referring to her
book on hell] from cover to cover so you can understand
more about hell and the hereafter."[9] She confidently declares: "The Spirit of the living God revealed to me everything I am telling you."[10]

The Horrors of Hell
and a Tour of Heaven

Mrs. Baxter believes that she was literally transported to
hell over a period of thirty days. There she observed people
being tormented, describing in detail what she saw ("their
decayed flesh [was] falling off their bones," "demons [were]
taking turns poking a soul with spears," "the fire burned my
body and the worms crawled over and through me," etc.).

She tells us that hell is in the center of the earth.[11] Jesus
took her through a "slinky-like" tunnel into hell which is
shaped like a human body and is divided into parts and
rooms. One room is called the "fun center" where there are
special torments for mediums, warlocks, witches and mind
readers. She implies that Satan is in charge of the "fun center."[12]

Visiting the "belly of hell," she learns that it is seven-
teen miles high and three miles around like a circle. "Jesus
gave me the exact measurements," she writes.[13] She is
even abandoned by Jesus in hell (twice!) and told by Him,
"My child, hell is real. But you could never know for sure
until you had experienced it for yourself."[14]

She sees a preacher in hell and is told he is there for his racism, for compromising the Word and for taking money from the poor.[15] She saw another preacher who was in torment partly because "he said the Holy Ghost baptism was a lie."[16]

She learns that paradise was once close to hell, but was moved when Christ died and rose again.[17] Hell used to be a holding tank for OT believers.[18] Baxter clearly teaches that one can lose one's salvation.[19]

In the ten days she was taken by Jesus to tour heaven, Baxter learned many things. She describes the gates, music, angels, activities, landscape and citizenry of heaven. She tells us that diamonds as large as blocks of concrete are used for the mansions of soulwinners. There is a "file room" where angels are scrutinizing people's lives for God's constant approval or disapproval.[20]

She learns that all children go to heaven, especially victims of abortion.[21] In fact, there is a special planet for aborted and stillborn babies as well as animals. She says that in heaven there is a hall of platinum with rooms full of unclaimed blessings for Christians.[22]

An Evaluation of Mrs. Baxter's Revelations

We must say at the outset that Mrs. Baxter seems genuinely concerned for the salvation of her readers. Yet her grasp of salvation is at times confused, and at other times seems close to a salvation by works.

Her calling exceeds that of the Apostles, for she not only writes "inspired" Scripture, she actually claims to have gone to heaven and hell. Her sense of being given information by Jesus is absolute. She does not say, "I had this impression in my spirit," but "*I went there! Jesus told me this!*" And she has the words of Jesus to her in quotation marks, indicating she wrote them down exactly as He said them to her.

Scripture, however, says that "the secret things belong to the LORD our God" (Deuteronomy 29:29) and warns us, "Do not go beyond what is written" (1 Corinthians 4:6). Mrs. Baxter must not believe that First Corinthians 2:9 applies to her: "No eye has seen, no ear has heard, no mind has conceived what God has prepared for those who love him." We are a people of the *ear* (we are to listen to the written Word of God, the Bible), not a people of the *eye*.

The reserve and reticence of the Bible to describe hell and heaven is replaced by Baxter's detailed descriptions of both realms. As one critic says, "The book [on hell] reads much more like an account of a horrible nightmare or a re-action to prescription drugs than it does the Bible."[23]

She indicates, contrary to Scripture, that people in hell are objects of Jesus' love, not of His wrath.[24] He wishes to let them out of hell, but it is too late. She writes, "Though those in hell were lost forever, I knew that He still loved them and would for all eternity."[25] Such well-intentioned sentiment does not have biblical support, for the "wrath of God abides on" all those who have rejected His Son (John 3:36, NASB).

The picture she gives us of Jesus (when He abandons her twice in hell) is that of a cosmic sadist. And her explanation that He did that so she could know hell's reality for herself is nothing other than unadulterated gnosticism (a heresy that claims that some believers can acquire "special knowledge"). As one critic points out, there is no way that Jesus would abandon a Christian in hell even for a moment, since the Bible is clear that the believer is not "appointed . . . to wrath" (1 Thessalonians 5:9, KJV; Romans 8:1).[26]

These narratives of short trips to hell and heaven are questionable as well because we learn from Luke 16:19-31 that no one can leave the place of torment and relocate to paradise, and we have no biblical evidence of someone coming back to earth after going to heaven, without dying. (The words "without dying" are important, for Lazarus in John 11 is an example, I believe, of one who passed through physical death and was returned to his earthly body by the resurrection power of the Savior.)

Paul says the glories of heaven are indescribable. Mrs. Baxter takes 205 pages to describe those glories. Paul got a "thorn in the flesh" for his revelations; all Mrs. Baxter appears to get are speaking engagements and book tours.

Knowing the Mind of God

Another troubling aspect of Baxter's revelations concerns healing. She declares that God always wants to heal every Christian: "Saints, the Lord has storehouses of blessings just for you. They are waiting in heaven for you to claim them and to receive them now, here on earth. God wants to save you. He wants to deliver you. He wants to heal you."[27] Yet despite her assurances that she knows what God "wants," her teaching on healing does not find biblical support. In Paul's situation, at least, God did *not* want to heal him of his thorn in the flesh (2 Corinthians 12:7-9).

Unbelief, Baxter says, is the only reason anyone is not healed; she quotes Jesus as saying to her,

> Healings are waiting for people on earth. The day will come when there will be an avalanche of miracles and healings on the earth. . . . The blessings

contained [in these storehouses] await the belief of those on earth. All they have to do is believe and receive—believe that I am the Lord Jesus Christ and that I am able to do these things, and receive My gifts.[28]

But in the case of the Apostle Paul, it was not that he didn't believe Christ *could* remove his thorn in the flesh— he was told that Christ *did not want to*.

Mrs. Baxter insists, "In heaven with perfect bodies, we will rest in Christ with no more pain or physical affliction." The Scriptures concur with that conclusion. But she adds, "Still, He also wants us to be healed now,"[29] with the implication that God cannot use us if we are physically impaired. "God doesn't desire that we spend our later years bedridden and ineffective," she writes. "He wants to keep us active and productive."[30] Tell that to saints who spend their latter years bedridden. Are they "ineffective"? Hardly. History is replete with examples of believers who accomplished great things for God while confined to a bed of sickness.

More Unbiblical Teaching

Baxter also reveals that there is in heaven a hall of platinum with rooms full of unclaimed blessings—miracles and healings which are not asked for by Christians. All we have to do, Baxter says, is "believe." This idea runs counter to the biblical teaching that we are to pray "Thy will be done" and "Not my will but thine," says G. Richard Fisher, a Christian author who has made a thorough study of Baxter's writings.[31]

"When it comes to salvation, Baxter sends a very confused and garbled message," says Fisher. She holds to a defi-

nite works/righteousness.[32] Her concept of God implies that
He has to learn things, which violates the biblical doctrine of
God's omniscience. Fisher concludes that "Baxter's God is
more at home in Mormonism than biblical Christianity."[33]

Some might say, "What's the big deal? Baxter's 'revelations' aren't really hurting anyone, are they?" Fisher responds, "Lest we forget: All of this is implied as coming
right from God! There are not supposed to be errors, mis-
takes, contradictions, aberrations or liberties taken."[34]
Concerning Baxter's book, one writer says, "It is a melange
of untested claims, fiction, imagination, out-of-context
Bible verses, error and even heresy. . . . It is a modern
metaphysical gnostic text."[35]

More or Less Than the Word?

As troubling as these erroneous teachings are, the main
problem I have with Baxter's books is that she claims to
know more about the afterlife than is given in the Scriptures. "Walking by sight," even by someone else's, is neither honoring to God nor showing respect for the Word of
God. Baxter gives us details beyond the clear teaching of
the Bible (the size of hell, the fate of babies, the thorny
theological issue regarding paradise). She claims to have
had an experience like the Apostle John in Revelation 4!

In this respect, Baxter sounds very much like the rich man
in Luke 16, who argues that his brothers had not been sufficiently warned by the Word of God. Her information is more
specific than the Bible, but far less trustworthy. Fisher concludes that she is attempting to upstage the Bible with her
extra-biblical revelations. "To think that Baxter's book can
give us more than God already has, is a not-so-subtle deni-

gration of the Scriptures. God has been holding out on us—at least until the coming of Mary Baxter."[36]

How serious is this issue, however? Are Baxter's extrabiblical details about heaven just harmless speculation, or is there a subtle danger lurking here? A.W. Tozer offers some wise counsel in this area:

> Whatever keeps me from my Bible is my enemy, however harmless it may appear to be. Whatever engages my attention when I should be meditating on God and things eternal does injury to my soul. . . . Let me accept anything else instead of the Scriptures and I have been cheated and robbed to my eternal confusion.[37]

Tozer also advises us to evaluate any spiritual experience—including visions and dreams—by God's Word:

> Whatever originates outside the Scriptures should for that very reason be suspect until it can be shown to be in accord with them. If it should be found to be contrary to the Word of revealed truth, no true Christian will accept it as being from God. However high the emotional content, no experience can be proved to be genuine unless we can find chapter and verse authority for it in the Scriptures. "To the word and to the testimony" must always be the last and final proof.[38]

Whenever Baxter refers to the Word of God, however, she appears to use it only to *validate*, not *evaluate*, her experiences. She writes, "I want you to understand that after I saw the heavenly creatures of God in my vision, I made a study

about them and discovered John's amazing description of
what I had witnessed in the book of Revelation."[39]

Giving Heed to Fables

In his article, "The 'Heavenly Hash' of Mary K. Baxter:
A Critical Look at Her Celestial Revelation,"[40] G. Richard
Fisher reminds us of Paul's command that we are to "teach
no other doctrine, neither give heed to fables" (1 Timothy
1:3-4, KJV). He points out that those who claim to have
taken trips to the other side contradict each other with
their extraordinary and fantastic claims. He recommends
William Alnor's *Heaven Can't Wait: A Survey of Alleged
Trips to the Other Side*[41] as a useful survey of such claims.

Fisher says that such "self-proclaimed heaven-hoppers"
are to be criticized for essentially arguing that Scripture is,
at best, ineffective in its ability to let the world know that
there is a heaven and there is a hell.[42] I completely concur
with his conclusion that "All we need to know about
heaven, and all that God wants us to know about heaven,
is contained in the Scriptures."[43]

Despite her intentions, Baxter is making a serious mistake
in going beyond Scripture. Fisher writes, "Trying to scare
people into heaven with vivid and imaginary scenes is coun-
terproductive and can produce skepticism when claims cannot be proved. . . . People need to stop visiting the bookstores
for the latest fads and crazes and revisit their Bibles."[44]

If we are to stick to the Scriptures when it comes to our
knowledge of the afterlife, the question immediately arises,
what exactly *does* the Bible say about heaven? In the next
chapter, we'll take a quick tour of our future home—not in a
vision or a dream, but between the pages of God's Word.

FIVE

Better Than Baxter: A Brief Survey of the Bible on Heaven

Heaven is not a state of mind. Heaven is reality itself. All that is fully real is Heavenly.

(C.S. Lewis, *The Great Divorce*)

One day when George MacDonald, the great Scottish preacher and writer, was talking with his son, the conversation turned to heaven and the prophet's version of the end of all things. "It seems too good to be true," the son said at one point. A smile crossed MacDonald's whiskered face. "Nay," he replied, "it is just so good it must be true."

(Philip Yancey, *Disappointment with God*)

Obviously excited, the elderly lady boarded the train and prepared for her first trip in years. Moving from seat to seat, she arranged and rearranged her belongings, and adjusted the window shade. Just when all was to her liking, the conductor called her destination. Surprised, she said, "Had I known the trip was so short, I wouldn't have wasted so much time."

Dear friends, now we are children of God, and
what we will be has not yet been made known. But we
know that when he appears, we shall be like him, for
we shall see him as he is.

(1 John 3:2)

A
s tempting as "firsthand" accounts of heaven
might be, we must go back to the Bible for authoritative truth about our future home. And when
we do, we learn that Baxter's "trip to heaven" and other
speculative accounts seem more like a sad grade-B movie,
missing the essence and subtlety of the original script. The
hypeless, fully orbed text of Scripture gives us all the information we really require about that next world.

The Old Testament

Although we can touch on only a few passages, it appears that the doctrine of the afterlife is not a primary concern of the Old Testament. Bible scholars speak of a
principle called *progressive revelation*, which teaches that
God does not give all that He wants us to know on a particular area of doctrine in one fell swoop. If one focuses
only on certain Old Testament texts, one could draw the
conclusion that a person sleeps in the grave after death
(Psalm 17:15; 31:17; 143:3) or that people cease to exist at
their physical deaths (Psalm 115:17; 88:10-12; 104:35).
Neither of these concepts is really taught in the Bible, but
those references (and a few others) have been used to
challenge the biblical doctrine of life after death. We need
to have a clear understanding of both the Old and New
Testament passages for the full doctrine of the afterlife.

The terms "heaven" and "the heavens" appear frequently in Scripture, though not all instances refer to the abode of God or the eternal destiny of the children of God. Our study will be more profitable if we divide the various uses of the term into several categories.

"Heaven" as a Part of Creation

A number of the Old Testament references to heaven have to do with God's great work of creation. The Bible begins with the words "in the beginning God created the *heavens* and the earth" (Genesis 1:1). In Genesis 14, Melchizedek blesses Abram, referring to God as "Creator of *heaven* and earth" (Genesis 14:19). The book of Exodus reminds us in the giving of the Ten Commandments that "in six days the LORD made the *heavens* and the earth . . ." (Exodus 20:11; cf. 31:17). Jeremiah also extols God's creativity: "He made the earth by his power; he founded the world by his wisdom and stretched out the *heavens* by his understanding" (Jeremiah 51:15).

Nehemiah 9:6 records the Levites praising God, saying, "You alone are the LORD. You made the *heavens*, even *the highest heavens*, and all their starry host, the earth and all that is on it, the seas and all that is in them. You give life to everything, and the multitudes of *heaven* worship you." This text seems to use the term "heaven" not only to refer to creation, but also to the place where the angels dwell in worship of the Creator.

So we see that "heaven," "the heavens," and even "the highest heavens" refer to that aspect of creation which is distinct from the earth, but was created along with the earth.

"Heaven" as God's Dwelling Place

The Old Testament clearly refers to heaven as the dwelling place of God. The angel of the Lord (thought by some scholars to be the Lord Himself) calls out to Abraham "from *heaven*" (Genesis 22:11, 15). Jacob's dream in which he saw angels ascending and descending on a stairway between heaven and earth caused him to exclaim, "This is none other than the house of God; this is the gate of *heaven*" (28:17).

Heaven as a place for *humans* to dwell is not as clearly stated. It appears from the early chapters of Genesis that God's original intention was that Adam and Eve would live forever in the garden. When sin entered in, God barred them from the tree of life, some biblical scholars suggest, to keep them from living in a perpetual state of sin (3:22). However, in Second Kings we are told that "the LORD was about to take Elijah up to *heaven* in a whirlwind" (2 Kings 2:1). Heaven is a place to which God was relocating His servant Elijah.

One is also reminded of the story of Enoch in Genesis 5:24, where we read, "Enoch walked with God; then he was no more, because God took him away." This is a problem passage for annihilationists (the wicked will eventually cease to exist). On the one hand, they argue that the expression "was no more" indicates the cessation of existence. But on the other hand, Genesis 5 indicates God's *pleasure* in Enoch—so why would God cause someone with whom He was pleased to "cease to exist"?

The answer is that God took Enoch to heaven. One preacher has paraphrased Genesis 5 as God saying, "Enoch, you've been walking with Me for many years. You know, we're closer to My home than to yours. Why don't you just come home with Me?" Heaven is God's home to which He escorted Enoch and snatched away Elijah.

Isaiah 66:1 tells us that "*Heaven* is my throne, and the earth is my footstool." Amos speaks of the Lord as the One who "builds his lofty palace in the *heavens* and sets its foundation on the earth" (Amos 9:6). Heaven is not only God's abode; it is the locality of His "lofty palace." One should not be surprised that Christians sing, "I've got a mansion, just over the hilltop" (cf. John 14:1-3).

"Heaven" as the Source of God's Blessings . . . or Judgment

Sometimes heaven is referred to in the Old Testament as the source of God's blessings or judgment. In an often arid, agricultural world, His blessing is as basic as rain. "The land you are crossing the Jordan to take possession of," says Moses in Deuteronomy 11:11, "is a land of mountains and valleys that drinks rain from *heaven*." The Lord will "shut *the heavens* so that it will not rain" if God's people fall into idolatry (Deuteronomy 11:17; cf. 1 Kings 8:35).

God provided His people with more than rain, declares Asaph, one of the writers of the Psalms. He reflects back upon God's provision for His people in the wilderness: "He gave a command to the skies above and opened the doors of the *heavens*; he rained down manna for the people to eat, he gave them the grain of *heaven*. Men ate the bread of angels" (Psalm 78:23-25; cf. 105:40).

Heaven is also the source of God's judgment. The burning sulfur which destroyed Sodom and Gomorrah in Genesis 19 came "from the LORD out of the *heavens*" (Genesis 19:24). When Hannah thanks the Lord for her son Samuel in First

Samuel 2:10, she prays that "those who oppose the LORD will be shattered. He will thunder against them from *heaven*; the LORD will judge the ends of the earth." King David speaks of God's *anger* in Second Samuel 22:8: "The earth trembled and quaked, the foundations of the *heavens* shook; they trembled because he was angry."

"Heaven" in Contrast or Connection with Earth

A number of Old Testament passages compare or contrast heaven and earth. In Deuteronomy 4 Moses says, "From *heaven* he made you hear his voice to discipline you. On earth he showed you his great fire, and you heard his words from out of the fire" (4:36). "To the LORD your God belong the *heavens*, even the *highest heavens*," says Moses, "the earth and everything in it" (10:14). Psalm 115:16 says, "The *highest heavens* belong to the LORD, but the earth he has given to man." David sees "the angel of the LORD standing between *heaven* and earth, with a drawn sword in his hand" (1 Chronicles 21:16). When God's people repent and call on God's name, God promises in Second Chronicles 7:14, "then will I hear from *heaven* and will forgive their sin and will heal their land."

Solomon declares in Proverbs, "As the *heavens* are high and the earth is deep, so the hearts of kings are unsearchable" (25:3). This same king "devoted [himself] to study and to explore by wisdom all that is done under *heaven*" (Ecclesiastes 1:13). Solomon cautions worshipers of God in the book of Ecclesiastes, "Do not be quick with your mouth, do not be hasty in your heart to utter anything before God. God is in *heaven* and you are on earth, so let your words be few" (5:2). Some scholars believe that Isaiah 14:12 speaks of Satan's expulsion from God's presence: "How you have fallen from *heaven*, O morning star, son of the dawn! You have been cast down to the earth." The Apostle Paul may have been thinking of Isaiah 14 when he wrote in Ephesians 2:2 of "the ruler of the kingdom of the air, the spirit who is now at work in those who are disobedient."

All of creation (both heaven and earth) is called to serve as a witness to earthly events or to praise God in a number of passages. Moses warns the people against idolatry by saying, "I call *heaven* and earth as witnesses against you this day" (Deuteronomy 4:26; cf. 30:19; 31:28). Job's friend Zophar lectures him about the wicked who will be severely judged by God: "The *heavens* will expose his guilt; the earth will rise up against him" (Job 20:27). David calls upon all creation to praise the Lord: "Let *heaven* and earth praise him, the seas and all that move in them" (Psalm 69:34). "Shout for joy, O *heavens*;" says Isaiah, "rejoice, O earth; burst into song, O mountains! For the LORD comforts his people and will have compassion on his afflicted ones" (49:13). Both parts of creation will rejoice over the downthrow of one of Israel's primary enemies, says Jeremiah: "Then *heaven* and earth and all that is in them will shout for joy over Babylon" (51:48).

"Heaven" as a Symbol of God's Glory or Mystery

Sometimes heaven is referred to in the Old Testament to emphasize God's glory or His mystery. There is a fascinating passage in Exodus 24 where we are told that Moses and Aaron "saw the God of Israel: and there was under his feet as it were a paved work of a sapphire stone, and as it were the body of *heaven* in his clearness" (Exodus 24:10, KJV). This verse perhaps contributes to the widespread belief that heaven will have streets of gold and precious stones. As his death approaches Moses blesses the tribe of Asher with the words, "There is no one like the God of Jeshurun, who rides on the *heavens* to help you and on the clouds in his majesty" (Deuteronomy 33:26).

In the book of Job we find that Job gets spiritually mugged by his friends when he begins to claim his innocence in the midst of his sufferings. Zophar says to him, "Can you fathom the mysteries of God? Can you probe the limits of the Almighty? They are higher than the *heavens*—what can you do? They are deeper than the depths of the grave—what can you know? Their measure is longer than the earth and wider than the sea" (Job 11:7-9). Job's buddy Eliphaz explains Job's trials by saying that he must submit to God and repent: "Is not God in the heights of *heaven*? And see how lofty are the highest stars!" (22:12). Job sarcastically responds to these "counselors" when he says, "How you have helped the powerless! . . . The pillars of the *heavens* quake, aghast at his rebuke" (26:2, 11).

Job is put in his place by the Lord, who finally breaks His silence in chapters 38-42. "Do you know the laws of the *heavens*? Can you set up God's dominion over the earth?" (38:33). God asks, "Who has the wisdom to count the clouds? Who can tip over the water jars of the *heavens* when the dust becomes hard and the clods of earth stick together?" (38:37-38). Although this reference is to rain, the specific point is that only God has the power to provide the earth with needed moisture.

"Heaven" and the Priority of Praise

The contemplation of heaven (either the galaxies or the abode of God) should lead one to wonder and praise. The Psalmist says that he takes the time to "consider your *heavens*, the work of your fingers," which causes him to ask, "what is man that you are mindful of him?" (Psalm 8:3-4). "The *heavens* declare the glory of God" (19:1), for they are "the work of [God's] hands" (102:25). David says, "Now I know that the LORD saves his anointed; he answers him from his holy *heaven* with the saving power of his right hand" (20:6). All human beings are to worship the Lord, the Psalmist insists: "Let them praise the name of the LORD, for his name alone is exalted; his splendor is above the earth and the *heavens*" (148:13).

The prophet Daniel records the confession of a pagan king in the fourth chapter of his book: "Now I, Nebuchadnezzar, praise and exalt and glorify the King of *heaven*, because everything he does is right and all his ways are just. And those who walk in pride he is able to humble" (4:37). Daniel criticizes King Belshazzar for not humbling himself before God: ". . . you have set yourself up against the Lord of *heaven*" (5:23). Daniel also testifies that he saw in a vision "one like a son of man, coming with the clouds of *heaven*" (7:13).

"Heaven" and the Attributes of God

Sometimes heaven is used as a literary device, especially to teach something about the character of God. In proclaiming God's *uniqueness*, Moses challenges Israel to "ask from one end of the *heavens* to the other" (Deuteronomy 4:32) to find out if there is any god who compares to the God of Israel. There is an intriguing promise in this same book of Deuteronomy where the Lord says that if Israel observes His word, then "your days and the days of your children may be many in the land that the LORD swore to give your forefathers, as many as the days that the *heavens* are above the earth" (11:21).

A key mention of heaven occurs in Solomon's dedication of the temple, when the king acknowledges that even the magnificent temple which Israel has built cannot "capture" God: "Will God really dwell on earth? The *heavens*, even the highest *heaven*, cannot contain you. How much less this temple I have built!" (1 Kings 8:27). Heaven is part of God's created order; it cannot "contain" God. Theologians sometimes use the term *transcendence* to indicate God's separateness from creation. Isaiah also speaks about this attribute of God in Isaiah 55:9: "As the *heavens* are higher than the earth, so are my ways higher than your ways and my thoughts than your thoughts."

David rejoices in the greatness of God's *love*, saying, "As high as the *heavens* are above the earth, so great is his love for those who fear him" (Psalm 103:11). He gives thanks for God's *faithfulness*: "For great is your love, higher than the *heavens*; your faithfulness reaches to the skies" (108:4). God's Word is "eternal" and "stands firm in the *heavens*" (119:89). God's *omnipresence* is highlighted in Psalm 139:8: "If I go up to the *heavens*, you are there." The Lord declares in Isaiah 66:1 that "*Heaven* is my throne, and the earth is my footstool." Jeremiah gives us an important reference to God's *immanence* (His being everywhere present in creation): "Do not I fill *heaven* and earth?" (Jeremiah 23:24). The Lord perhaps uses hyperbole (an exaggeration for effect) in Jeremiah 31:37 when He speaks of His *trustworthiness*: " 'Only if the *heavens* above can be measured and the foundations of the earth below be searched out will I reject all the descendants of Israel because of all they have done,' declares the LORD." A similar statement occurs in 33:25-26: "If I have not established my covenant with day and night and the fixed laws of *heaven* and earth, then I will reject the descendants of Jacob."

"Heaven" and Its Replacement

The Old Testament also teaches that there will be new heavens and a new earth. Isaiah says that there will come a time when "the *heavens* will vanish like smoke, the earth will wear out like a garment" (Isaiah 51:6). "Behold, I will create," says the Lord in Isaiah 65:17, "new *heavens* and a new earth. The former things will not be remembered, nor will they come to mind." The Creator, who rested from the work of creation on the seventh day (Genesis 2:3), will create again!

A Summary of the Old Testament on Heaven

The emphasis in the Old Testament seems to be primarily on living this life for God, not focusing on the next life in heaven. Belief in an afterlife is shown in passages such as Second Samuel 12:23, where David reflects on the death of his illegitimate son by Bathsheba: "I will go to him, but he will not return to me." Daniel 12:2 teaches us that "Multitudes who sleep in the dust of the earth will awake: some to everlasting life, others to shame and everlasting contempt." The Psalmist declares in Psalm 23:6 that he will "dwell in the house of the LORD forever."

The term "heaven" has many uses in the Old Testament. Sometimes it refers to the source of rain (that is, the atmosphere), but more frequently is used to indicate that aspect of creation which is not the earth. Heaven is God's dwelling place, the location of His home and His lofty palace, but it cannot contain God. In a unique sense heaven belongs to the Lord, while earth is described as having been given to man. Heaven is called upon to witness the acts of man on earth and is commanded to shout for joy at the good things which the Creator does for man. Heaven declares God's glory and demonstrates His splendor. God's characteristics (attributes) of uniqueness, immanence, transcendence, faithfulness, trustworthiness, love and omnipresence are brought into view by a number of references to heaven.

The fullness of the doctrine of heaven is unfolded only when one comes to the New Testament. While several Old Testament ideas are repeated, some new concepts are introduced.

The New Testament

One reference to heaven in the New Testament emphasizes the absolute authority of Jesus' words. He says in Matthew 24:35, "*Heaven* and earth will pass away, but my words will never pass away." We also see in the New Testament that heaven is the dwelling place of God. Jesus taught His disciples to pray, "Our Father in *heaven* . . ." (6:9). It is a literal place, for Christians are to "store up for [themselves] treasures in *heaven*, where moth and rust do not destroy, and where thieves do not break in and steal" (6:20). We are told in Psalm 123:1 that God's throne is "in heaven," but Matthew 5:34 clarifies that heaven itself *is* God's throne.

Our Effect on Heaven

There is a direct connection between the heavenly realm and this one with regard to "binding and loosing," as Jesus states in Matthew 16:19: "I will give you the keys of the kingdom of *heaven*; whatever you bind on earth will be bound in *heaven*, and whatever you loose on earth will be loosed in *heaven.*" Roman Catholic doctrine uses this verse to teach the authority of Peter as the first pope; however, the text suggests that *every* believer in Jesus Christ has the authority from God to declare sins forgiven ("loosed") or unforgiven ("bound") based on a person's response to the gospel.

A Camel and the Kingdom of Heaven

Jesus says in Matthew 19:23-24 that ". . . it is hard for a rich man to enter the kingdom of *heaven.* . . . It is easier for a camel to go through the eye of a needle than for a rich man to enter the kingdom of God." I've heard preachers say that the "eye of the needle" was a low gate into Jerusalem and that a camel carrying a burden would have to crawl on its knees through that gate. This, they say, is a picture of the need for repentance if one is to enter the kingdom of God.

It's a nice explanation; the only problem with this interpretation is that *there is no such gate in Jerusalem.* Besides, the Greek word used for "camel" literally means "camel" and the Greek word used for "eye of the needle" literally refers to the eye of a *sewing* needle. Jesus' point is not that it is hard to stuff a camel through the eye of a sewing needle (I wonder which hump you would shove through first?), but that it is *impossible.* Getting into the kingdom of heaven does not depend upon any efforts of finite man. And those with riches, although thought by Jewish society to be closer to God, cannot make it into God's kingdom without God's grace.

Jesus promises in the Beatitudes, "Blessed are the poor in spirit, for theirs is the kingdom of *heaven*" (Matthew 5:3). We are also told in verse 10, "Blessed are those who are persecuted because of righteousness, for theirs is the kingdom of *heaven.*" This life determines one's place in that life.

Sheep, Goats, and the Kingdom of Heaven

Matthew 25 teaches that the "sheep," those believers who knew Christ and lived for him, will be invited by Christ to "take your inheritance, the kingdom prepared for you since the creation of the world" (25:34). The "goats," those who were not saved and showed their lack of salvation by the way they lived, will be told by Christ, "depart from me, you who are cursed, into the eternal fire prepared for the devil and his angels" (25:41). Although the terms "heaven" or "hell" are not used in Matthew 25, it is clear that Jesus is speaking about the only two destinies of man, for verse 46 reads, "Then they [the "goats"] will go away to eternal punishment, but the righteous [the "sheep"] to eternal life."

Heaven: Jesus' Former Residence

The Gospel of John highlights the deity of the Lord Jesus Christ, declaring in chapter 1: "'I tell you the truth, you shall see *heaven* open, and the angels of God ascending and descending on the Son of Man" (1:51). The Spirit of God who was to "come down from *heaven*" would appear on Christ, John 1:32 tells us. The majority of the references in John's Gospel to heaven occurs in chapters 3 and 6. Jesus declares that heaven was His home in John 3:13: "No one has ever gone into *heaven* except the one who came from *heaven*—the Son of Man" (cf. 3:31). "[I]t is not Moses who has given you the bread from *heaven*," declares Jesus, "but it is my Father who gives you the true bread from *heaven*. For the bread of God is he who comes down from *heaven* and gives life to the world" (6:32-33). Jesus states, "I have come down from *heaven* not to do my will but to do the will of him who sent me" (6:38; cf. 6:42). First Corinthians 15:47 affirms the heavenly origin of Jesus, adding that "just as we have borne the likeness of the earthly man, so shall we bear the likeness of the man from *heaven*" (15:49). We are told in John 14:2-3 that Jesus has gone back to the Father's house to prepare places for His people and will be returning for them at some point in the future.

Heaven: Jesus' Present Location

The book of Acts begins by reminding the disciples who are staring at Jesus ascending into heaven that He will return "in the same way you have seen him go into *heaven*" (1:11). Heaven is a destination to which Jesus has gone and from which He will return. Peter proclaims in his Pentecost sermon that Jesus is the fulfillment of David's prophecy about God not abandoning His Holy One to decay. David proclaims, "You have made known to me the paths of life; you will fill me with joy in your presence" (2:28; Psalm 16:11). In his sermon after the healing of the crippled beggar, Peter challenges the Jews to repent, so "that times of refreshing may come from the Lord, and that he may send the Christ, who has been appointed for you—even Jesus. He must remain in *heaven* until the time comes for God to restore everything . . ." (3:19-21). God gives Peter a vision in Acts 10 to lead him to share the gospel with the Gentiles. The text says, "He saw *heaven* opened and something like a large sheet being let down to earth by its four corners . . ." (10:11). One is reminded of John's vision in Revelation 19: "I saw *heaven* standing open and there before me was a white horse, whose rider is called Faithful and True" (19:11).

Heaven and the End Times

Although there are various opinions on this most mysterious book in the Bible, John's "revelation of Jesus Christ"

promises a blessing to all who read it, hear it, take it to heart,
and keep it (1:3; 22:7). A quick reading of Revelation speaks
of five promises to be realized by God's people as they anticipate the real heaven.

First, please notice that there is *the Christ to be seen*. This
same apostle John tells us in First John 3 about the future
event when Christians will "see him as he is" (1 John 3:2).
John's revelation describes that actually taking place! In
Revelation 5 we read, "Then one of the elders said to me,
'Do not weep! See, the Lion of the tribe of Judah, the Root of
David, has triumphed. He is able to open the scroll and its
seven seals.' Then I saw a Lamb, looking as if it had been
slain . . ." (5:5-6).

Second, there will be *the new community to be enjoyed*.
We learn that there will be eating in heaven (most men
appreciate this fact), indicating fellowship and closeness
with Christ and His redeemed people. John writes, "To
him who overcomes, I will give the right to eat from the
tree of life, which is in the paradise of God" (2:7). To the
church in Pergamum John writes, "To him who overcomes, I will give some of the hidden manna" (2:17). Because believers will celebrate the wedding supper of the
Lamb (19:7, 9), heaven will be eternity's greatest party.

We will be dressed in white (symbolizing our purity in
Christ). To the church in Sardis John writes, "He who overcomes will . . . be dressed in white" (3:5). John sees under the
altar of God the souls of those who had been martyred because of the Word of God. "Then each of them was given a
white robe . . ." (6:11). In chapter 7 John sees "a great multi-
tude that no one could count, from every nation, tribe, people and language, standing before the throne and in front of
the Lamb. They were wearing white robes . . ." (7:9). The

ones wearing the white robes "are they who have come out of the great tribulation; they have washed their robes and made them white in the blood of the Lamb" (7:14).

We also learn that we will get new names! To the church in Pergamum John writes, "I will also give him a white stone with a new name written on it, known only to him who receives it" (2:17). To the church in Philadelphia John says, "I will write on him the name of my God . . . and I will also write on him my new name" (3:12).

And of course, there will be tremendous music in heaven. John tells us that when the Lamb took the scroll in chapter 5, "the four living creatures and the twenty-four elders fell down before the Lamb. Each one had a harp . . . and they sang a new song . . ." (5:8-9). In chapter 14 we read of the 144,000 who will stand with the Lamb on Mount Zion. John says, "I heard a sound from heaven . . . [which] was like that of harpists playing their harps. And they sang a new song before the throne . . ." (14:2-3). In chapter 15 we read that those who had been victorious over the beast and his image "held harps given them by God and sang the song of Moses the servant of God and the song of the Lamb . . ." (15:2-3; see also 18:22 regarding harpists). The angels, numbering thousands upon thousands, and ten thousand times ten thousand, will "[encircle] the throne and . . . in a loud voice [will sing]: 'Worthy is the Lamb, who was slain . . .' " (5:11-12). "Then I heard," John writes, "every creature in heaven and on earth and under the earth and on the sea, and all that is in them, singing: 'To him who sits on the throne and to the Lamb be praise and honor and glory and power, for ever and ever!' " (5:13).

Third, there will be *catastrophes to observe*. Much of the book of Revelation deals with the judgments which will be executed against the earth. Some no doubt will take place before the Second Coming of Christ. Chapter 6 speaks of the Lamb beginning to open the seals of judgment against the earth. These involve causing men to slay one another, the bringing of plagues and famine upon the earth, wild beasts unleashed on the earth, and a great earthquake. All earth's inhabitants beg the mountains to fall on them and to hide them from the wrath of the Lamb (6:4, 8, 12, 15-16). An angel hurls fire from the altar in heaven onto the earth, bringing peals of thunder, rumblings, flashes of lightning and an earthquake (8:5). A number of judgments follow, but do not lead to repentance among those being judged (9:20-21; cf. 16:9, 11, 21).

There will be war in heaven; Michael and his archangels will fight against the dragon and his angels (12:7). We read of the "fiery lake of burning sulfur" in 19:20. Satan will be bound for a thousand years and thrown into the Abyss (20:1-3). After that time he will be released and will make war against God, but will be defeated and thrown with the beast and the false prophet into the lake of burning sulfur to "be tormented day and night for ever and ever" (20:7-10).

All the wicked dead appear before the great white throne judgment (20:11-15), but it will be revealed that none of their names appear in the book of life. They will be thrown into the fiery lake of burning sulfur which is the second death (21:8; cf. 20:14). There is an "outside" to the kingdom of God and it is to that place that "the dogs, those who practice magic arts, the sexually immoral, the murderers, the idolaters and everyone who loves and practices falsehood" (22:15) will be eternally exiled.

One of the judgments to take place will be the judgment seat of Christ, described not in this book of Revelation, but in Second Corinthians 5:10 and Romans 14:10. The Christian rejoices at Revelation's teaching that although there will be tears in heaven, God "will wipe every tear from their eyes. There will be no more death or mourning or crying or pain, for the old order of things has passed away" (21:4).

Fourth, there will be *crowns to receive*. John writes (specifically to the church in Smyrna), "Be faithful, even to the point of death, and I will give you the crown of life" (2:10). Jesus says, "I am coming soon. Hold on to what you have, so that no one will take your crown" (3:11). We learn in chapter 4 that the twenty-four elders will "fall down before him who sits on the throne, and [will] worship him who lives for ever and ever. They [will] lay their crowns before the throne and say: 'You are worthy, our Lord and God . . .' " (4:10-11). Presumably some of those crowns will be distributed at the judgment seat of Christ, but will be joyfully cast in adoration at the Savior's feet by all the redeemed.

Fifth, there will be *a conquered world* to rule. We will reign and rule with Christ over the new heavens and the new earth. John dedicates Revelation in the first chapter "To him who loves us and has freed us from our sins by his blood, and has made us to be a kingdom and priests to serve his God and Father . . ." (1:5-6). "To him who overcomes and does my will to the end," John says to the church in Thyatira, "I will give authority over the nations" (2:26). Unbelievers will be forced to bow before God's people: "I will make those who are of the synagogue of Satan, who claim to be Jews though they are not, but are liars—I will make them come and fall down at your feet and acknowledge that I have loved you" (3:9). To the church in Laodicea John writes, "To him who overcomes, I will give the right to sit with me on my throne, just as I overcame and sat down with my Father on his throne" (3:21).

We read of the Lamb in chapter 5: "[Y]ou purchased men for God from every tribe and language and people and nation. You have made them to be a kingdom and priests to serve our God, and they will reign on the earth" (5:9-10). Those who had not worshiped the beast or his image "came to life and reigned with Christ a thousand years" (20:4). The "second death" has no power over those who participate in the "first resurrection," but they will be "priests of God and of Christ and will reign with him for a thousand years" (20:5-6). God's servants "will reign for ever and ever" (22:5).

In chapter 21 we learn that the first heaven and earth have passed away (21:1). The new Jerusalem has the appearance of a jewel (21:11), "of pure gold, as pure as glass" (21:18). The twelve gates will be twelve pearls, each gate made of a single pearl (21:21). "The great street of the city was of pure gold, like transparent glass" (21:21). There will be no need of temple, or sun, or moon, for their places are taken by the Lord God Almighty and the Lamb (21:22-23). There will be no night there (21:25; 22:5). No sin will be allowed in the new Jerusalem and its human inhabitants are only "those whose names are written in the Lamb's book of life" (21:27). In chapter 22 we read of the "river of the water of life . . . flowing from the throne of God and of the Lamb" (22:1). The "tree of life" stands on either side of the river, yielding its fruit every month. "Blessed are those who wash their robes, that they may have the right to the tree of life . . ." (22:14). The invitation is offered: "Whoever is thirsty, let him come; and whoever wishes, let him take the free gift of the water of life" (22:17).

A Summary of Our Brief Study

In summary, we learn that heaven is presented in the Old Testament as the source of some of God's blessings and His judgments. Much is made of the fact that heaven was created by God and is His dwelling place. Heaven is often contrasted with earth in the Old Testament, and references to heaven highlight certain attributes of God, especially His glory. There will be new heavens and a new earth, the Old Testament teaches.

The New Testament's references to heaven are far-ranging. We are told that heaven is the dwelling place of God and the place from which the Son of God has come to earth and where He now is located. We are told to live this life in light of that next one and encouraged to "bank" our treasures in heaven rather than on earth. Our preaching of the gospel on earth has an effect on heaven. And we are told to wait for the Lord Jesus Christ to return to take away His bride to her heavenly home. We learn a great deal about the events that await the child of God in the book of Revelation. In light of all this truth, what further revelations do we need?

SIX

Heaven Came Down

The story is told of a little girl vacationing with her parents in the mountains. As she tried to get to sleep on the top bunk, she heard thunder and became frightened.

"Mommy, I'm scared!"

"It's OK, dear," her mother said. "God is with you."

A few moments passed. "Mommy," the little voice said, "I want someone up here with skin on 'em!"

We did not follow cleverly invented stories when we told you about the power and coming of our Lord Jesus Christ, but we were eyewitnesses of his majesty.

(2 Peter 1:16)

The Word became flesh and made his dwelling among us. We have seen his glory, the glory of the One and Only, who came from the Father, full of grace and truth.

(John 1:14)

W e saw in a previous chapter that some are not content with the biblical material on heaven, insisting that they have had a personal tour. But such professed experiences, with their sensational, and, at times unscriptural, detail about the afterlife, cannot compete with the Word of God. One particular episode in the earthly life of the Lord Jesus reminds us of our heavenly home. And this story is fully trustworthy.

If there had been a daily newspaper in heaven, the headlines on the day the Second Person of the Trinity came to earth to be born of the Virgin Mary might have read: "Heaven Emptied! The Son Goes to Do the Father's Will!" Not only was heaven emptied, but Philippians 2 indicates that the Son of God emptied *Himself* in becoming human, in taking the position of a servant who would go through death on a cross to redeem sinners.

The term "incarnation" means "to become flesh," and that is precisely what the Son of God did. He took upon Himself a sinless human nature (including body, soul, mind, emotions and will) in order to become the perfect sacrifice for man's sins. But why was the Incarnation necessary?

The church scholar Anselm (c. 1033-1109) asked the same question and wrote the tract entitled *Cur Deus Homo?* Now if your Latin is as bad as mine, you need a translation. But before I translate that title for you, I want to tell you why Anselm wrote his little book. He was convinced that man had so violated the honor of God by his sin that he could never make up for his failure or ever satisfy the offended majesty of the Creator. Man owed a debt to God that man, even if given all eternity, could never repay. The debt is so overwhelming that only God could pay that debt. But God did not owe that debt—so why should *He* pay it? *How* could He pay it?

The answer, of course, was that God in His infinite love sent His fully divine Son down to earth to become man without ceasing to be God. The title of Anselm's work? *Why the God-Man?* We needed the God-Man to pay our debt.

I love the way music often communicates profound theological concepts, sometimes in a quite memorable fashion. One of the older choruses Christians sing seems almost to have been written by Anselm.

> He paid a debt He did not owe,
> I owed a debt I could not pay,
> I needed Someone to wash my sins away.
> And now I sing a brand new song—
>   "Amazing Grace"!
> Christ Jesus paid a debt that I could never pay.[1]

Forevermore Jesus Christ is the God-Man. That "visitor from heaven" looked like any other Jewish man of His day, suffered like other men of His time, and died a human death on the cross. Apart from His miracles and His marvelous words, was there any particular event in the earthly life of Jesus that shows that He was from another world?

A Transforming Transfiguration

The answer, according to the Scriptures, is yes. We read of the event known as the Transfiguration in Matthew 17:2-9, Mark 9:2-10, and Luke 9:28-36. Using Luke's account as our primary focus, we see that Jesus has just predicted his murder at the hands of the religious authorities, an execution to be followed by His glorious resurrection (9:22). He then challenges His disciples to take up their crosses and follow Him.

Contrasting this world with the next, Jesus asks the now famous question, "What good is it for a man to gain the whole world, and yet lose or forfeit his very self?" (9:25). This contrast of "gaining the whole world" versus "losing one's soul" certainly indicates two competing worlds, the second of which will be marked by the singular test as to what one has done in the first world with Jesus Christ.

Jesus then warns: "If anyone is ashamed of me and my words, the Son of Man will be ashamed of him when he comes in his glory and in the glory of the Father and of the holy angels" (9:26). The contrast between this first world and the next is quite clear. This first world is characterized as a place which sorely tempts the believer to be ashamed of Christ and His words. The next world entails the coming of the "Son of Man" in His glory. In that coming He will respond with shame where He finds shame.

Jesus then gives a rather enigmatic statement, apparently about the disciples: "I tell you the truth, some who are standing here will not taste death before they see the kingdom of God" (9:27). The word for "taste" in Greek can mean "partake of, enjoy, come to know something."[2] So Jesus has said that there are some standing here who will not experience death before they see the kingdom of God. But what does this statement mean?

An Interpretative Menu

Several suggestions have been made. Among them are the ideas that the disciples would not die until they saw (1) the coming of God's kingdom in the resurrection of Jesus; (2) the coming of God's kingdom in the Spirit's coming at Pentecost; (3) the spread of the church throughout the world;

(4) the recognition that the kingdom has already come in
the Person of the Son; (5) Jerusalem's destruction in A.D. 70;
(6) the Second Coming of the Lord; or (7) the event known
as the Transfiguration.[3] It seems quite reasonable, suggests
one New Testament scholar, that the promise of Luke 9:27
is understood by Luke as having been fulfilled in the very
next event—the transfiguration.[4]

Jesus' astounding statement *is* immediately followed by
the event known as the Transfiguration. Let us carefully
observe what took place there.

The Appearance of Jesus

Jesus takes the Three (Peter, John and James) up onto a
mountain "to pray" (9:28). As Peter, James and John are
on the mountain with Jesus, He becomes "transfigured"
before them. The Greek word for "transfigured" is the root
of our English word "metamorphosis" and is used by both
Matthew and Mark to describe the change in Jesus (Luke
simply says that the appearance of His face "became different" [9:29, NASB]). This Greek term is used in only four
places in the New Testament: in Matthew 17:2 and its
parallel; Mark 9:2, in Second Corinthians 3:18, and in
Romans 12:2. The term means to "transform, change in
form"[5] and can refer to two different types of changes: (1)
one that is outwardly visible, specifically that "of Jesus,
who took on the form of his heavenly glory and *was transfigured*," or (2) "of a transformation invisible to the physical eye."[6] Both Second Corinthians 3:18 ("And we, who
with unveiled faces all reflect the Lord's glory, are *being
transformed* into his likeness with ever-increasing glory,
which comes from the Lord, who is the Spirit") and
Romans 12:2 ("Do not conform any longer to the pattern

of this world, but *be transformed* by the renewing of your mind. Then you will be able to test and approve what God's will is—his good, pleasing and perfect will") relate to a transformation which is invisible to the physical eye.

"Whiter Than White"

Two specific changes occur to Jesus that are seen by the three disciples. The first change in this transfiguration concerns His face. We are told that His face "shone like the sun" (Matthew 17:2). Luke says that "the appearance of his face changed," while Mark's Gospel makes no comment about the face of Jesus.

The second change involved Jesus' clothes. Matthew says "his clothes became as white as the light" (17:2). Mark says "his clothes became dazzling white, whiter than anyone in the world could bleach them" (9:3). The term used for "white" has a verb form, which is used in Revelation 7:14 to refer to those who "have washed their robes and made them *white* in the blood of the Lamb." Mark says that no "bleacher" or "one who cleans woolen cloth"[7] could get His clothes any whiter.

The term "radiant" or "dazzling" is used only here in Mark in the New Testament and was used in the Greek translation of the Old Testament to refer to the radiance of stars or the luster of metals.[8] Luke uses a different word picture in describing Jesus' clothes. He says that they "became as bright as a flash of lightning" (Luke 9:29), an expression used nowhere else in the New Testament.

Two Glorious Friends

The four on the mountain (Jesus, Peter, James and John) are joined by two others: Moses and Elijah, the Old

Testament heroes of the faith. These two men represent the law (Moses) and the prophets (Elijah). Matthew says that "just then there appeared before them Moses and Elijah, talking with Jesus" (Matthew 17:3).

Luke gives us a bit more detail when he says "two *men*, Moses and Elijah, appeared in glorious splendor, talking with Jesus. They spoke about his departure, which he was about to bring to fulfillment at Jerusalem" (9:30-31). Luke does not use the ordinary word for "man" that could be translated "person," but a special word meaning man in contrast to woman, or man in contrast to boy.[9] Perhaps Luke wants to make it clear these two were not angels *in the form of* men; these were actual men—human beings.

The phrase, "appeared in glorious splendor" can be literally translated, "The ones who appeared or became visible in glory." One Greek dictionary suggests that this expression is used "mostly of beings that make their appearance in a supernatural manner."[10] It is significant that Peter, James and John not only see Jesus in His glory, but also Moses and Elijah in "glorious splendor."

The Topic of Conversation

Only Luke's Gospel specifies what the topic of conversation between Jesus, Moses and Elijah was: "They spoke about his *departure*, which he was about to bring to fulfillment at Jerusalem" (9:31). The term "departure" is the Greek word *exodos* which can refer to the Exodus, Israel's rescue from Egypt (Hebrews 11:22), or can be used euphemistically to mean one's death (2 Peter 1:15).[11] His death is obviously what is meant here in Luke 9:31.

Note that Christ's "exodus" is something which He was about "to bring about" (literally, "to fulfill or complete").

Lest anyone think that Jesus was solely a *victim* in the events surrounding Calvary, the Scriptures are clear, as Jesus Himself said, that "no one takes [my life] from me, but I lay it down of my own accord. I have authority to lay it down and authority to take it up again" (John 10:18).

Luke tells us that Moses and Elijah were discussing Jesus' "departure" or death which He was "about to bring to fulfillment at Jerusalem" (Luke 9:31). Apparently these Old Testament saints who only looked forward to the redeeming work of the Messiah (1 Peter 1:10-11) now in glory understood what was about to take place in human history by Christ. One New Testament scholar suggests that the term "exodos" here in Luke 9:31 refers to the whole complex of Jesus' saving work: His death, resurrection and ascension.[12]

A Well-Intentioned, Yet Erroneous, Suggestion

In comparing the three Gospel accounts of what happened next, it appears that Peter, James and John "were very sleepy" (Luke 9:32). As they became fully awake, Luke tells us, "they saw his glory and the two men standing with him" (9:32). Do not miss the fact that the three see "his glory." John says in the first chapter of his Gospel, "We have seen *his glory*, the glory of the One and Only, who came from the Father, full of grace and truth" (John 1:14).

The transfiguration of Christ was a *transforming* event for Peter, James and John. Peter refers to it in Second Peter 1:16: "We did not follow cleverly invented stories when we told you about the power and coming of our Lord Jesus Christ, but we were eyewitnesses of his majesty." He is not referring to the resurrection or the ascension of the Lord, but the *transfiguration*, as the next two verses show:

> For he received honor and glory from God the Father when the voice came to him from the Majestic Glory, saying, "This is my Son, whom I love; with him I am well pleased." We ourselves heard this voice that came from heaven when we were with him on the sacred mountain. (1:17-18)

John 1:14 is probably John's reflection back on the event of the transfiguration as well: "The Word became flesh and made his dwelling among us. We have seen his glory, the glory of the One and Only, who came from the Father, full of grace and truth." The expression "made his dwelling" is the verb form of the noun Peter used when he said, "I will put up three *shelters*" (Matthew 17:4). What Peter needed to learn was that God had made His dwelling with us; we do not need to build Him a tent to live in!

As for James, we do not have a written account from him about the transfiguration. This James, of course, is not the same person who wrote the epistle of James. The James who experienced the wonder of the transfiguration is the one who was put to death by Herod Antipas as recorded for us in Acts 12:2.

Luke's Gospel provides some interesting insights on Peter's outburst, which occurred when Moses and Elijah "were leaving Jesus" (9:33). This is the only place in the New Testament where this Greek verb for "leaving" is used; it seems to have the idea of separating something from something else, though it can simply mean to go away.[13] At this point, Peter speaks up. Apparently, he intends to keep Moses and Elijah from leaving; Peter wants the experience to continue.

Peter addresses Jesus and states, "Master, it is good for us to be here. Let us put up three shelters—one for you, one for Moses and one for Elijah" (Luke 9:33). Significantly, Luke quotes Peter as using the term "Master," rather than the normal word for teacher. One scholar says, "Whereas the title 'teacher' in Luke was used of Jesus only by strangers, 'Master' was used only by Jesus' followers and reveals better his authority and might."[14]

This term "shelter" can mean "tent, booth, lodging, dwelling,"[15] and often implies the heavenly realm. For example, it is used in Luke 16:9 where Jesus challenges His disciples: "I tell you, use worldly wealth to gain friends for yourselves, so that when it is gone, you will be welcomed into eternal *dwellings*." This term is used of God's "dwelling place" in Revelation 13:6 ("[The beast] opened his mouth to blaspheme God, and to slander his name and his *dwelling place* and those who live in heaven"). It is also used of the New Jerusalem described in Revelation 21:3, where we read, "Now the *dwelling* of God is with men, and he will live with them. They will be his people, and God himself will be with them and be their God."

Could this be another occasion where Peter (inadvertently) is trying to get Jesus to bypass the cross? Peter wants to set up "dwellings" now. Moses and Elijah knew that Jesus must accomplish His "departure." The "dwellings" were to come *after* the "exodus"! One New Testament commentator suggests that

> Peter wants to mark the occasion by holding a Feast of Tabernacles (in which the Jews lived in tent-like shelters for seven days as a way of reenacting the exodus from Egypt and wanderings in the wilderness. See Lev. 23:42-44). But it is wrong for Peter to want to keep Moses and Elijah in this

way. He would be making Jesus just one more episode in the history of Israel; but Jesus *is* Israel per-
sonified, and it is time for Moses and Elijah to give
way. What they had helped to create has appeared in the person of Jesus.[16]

Stein points out that "such huts were constructed at the
festival of tabernacles/booths (Leviticus 23:33-43; Exodus
23:16; 34:22; Deuteronomy 16:13-16). In Luke 16:9 the
same Greek term is used in referring to the final state of the
righteous as 'eternal dwellings.' "[17]

Peter's proposal was, as one commentator puts it, "a most
unfortunate suggestion. Not only did it imply putting Moses
and Elijah on a level with Christ, but it would have impeded
and delayed the very going which had been planned from
eternity and for which the time had now come."[18] Certainly
Peter felt he was complimenting Jesus by putting Him in the
same class as the great Old Testament luminaries Moses and
Elijah. But his well-intentioned compliment was actually a
denigration of the Son of God. "Peter erred in equating Jesus
with Moses and Elijah. They were not equals."[19]

A Cloud of Knowing

Peter was right that it was good for them to be there, but
probably for the wrong reasons. He is immediately cor-
rected by a divine voice from heaven. God the Father in-
terrupts Peter's excited building plans by two specific
attention-getters. First, a bright cloud envelops them,
gripping them with fear (the cloud is described by Matthew as "full of light, illuminated").[20] A bright cloud indi-
cated the very presence of God in the Old Testament. In
Exodus 13:21 we read that "By day the LORD went ahead

of them in a pillar of *cloud* to guide them on their way and by night in a pillar of fire to give them light, so that they could travel by day or night." When speaking about the end of the world, Jesus said, "At that time they will see the Son of Man coming in *a cloud* with power and great glory" (Luke 21:27). Daniel prophesies:

> In my vision at night I looked, and there before me was one like a son of man, coming with *the clouds* of heaven. He approached the Ancient of Days and was led into his presence. He was given authority, glory and sovereign power; all peoples, nations and men of every language worshiped him. His dominion is an everlasting dominion that will not pass away, and his kingdom is one that will never be destroyed. (Daniel 7:13-14)

There should be no doubt that the One of whom Daniel speaks is equal to God!

Jesus says to Caiaphas the high priest (just before the Lord's crucifixion): "In the future you will see the Son of Man sitting at the right hand of the Mighty One and coming on *the clouds* of heaven" (Matthew 26:64). Believers who are alive at the Second Coming of the Lord will be "caught up . . . *in the clouds* to meet the Lord in the air. And so we will be with the Lord forever" (1 Thessalonians 4:17). John begins his book of Revelation with the words: "Look, he is coming *with the clouds*, and every eye will see him, even those who pierced him; and all the peoples of the earth will mourn because of him. So shall it be! Amen" (Revelation 1:7). As the cloud "enveloped" Peter, James and John, they became fearful.

The second attention-getter used by the Father is a "voice from the cloud," saying, "This is my Son, whom I love; with him I am well pleased. Listen to him!" (Matthew 17:5). Luke's account differs slightly by reporting that the voice says, "This is my Son, *whom I have chosen*; listen to him" (Luke 9:35).

Only Matthew tells us that the three disciples "fell facedown to the ground, terrified" when they heard the voice from the cloud (Matthew 17:6). I understand there is one television preacher who, in the middle of preaching, will cock his head to the side and say, "Yes, Father? Yes, Father. I will tell them!" Beware of any such preacher who acts as if he is receiving direct communication from God.

But in this case, there *is* direct communication from God. When the Father speaks here, His words are to the point: "Listen to my Son!" Peter is told to listen even as he is in the middle of talking.

Before refrigeration, people used icehouses to preserve their food. Icehouses had thick walls, no windows and a tightly fitted door. In winter, when lakes were frozen, large blocks of ice were cut, hauled to the icehouse and covered with sawdust, lasting well into the summer. The story is told of one man who lost a valuable watch while working in such an icehouse. He searched and searched for it, carefully raking through the sawdust, but could not find it. His friends also helped look, but they too were unsuccessful. A small boy, hearing about the fruitless search, slipped into the icehouse during the noon hour and soon came out with the watch. Amazed, the men asked how he found it. "I closed the door," the boy replied, "lay down on the sawdust and kept very still. Soon, I heard the watch ticking."

We Christians find it awfully hard to keep very still and listen. But Peter needed to do just that, for he was in grave danger of missing the entire point of the transfiguration of God's Son.

Lessons from the Transfiguration

The most obvious lesson from the event known as the transfiguration is that there is another world beyond this one. The two key figures of Moses and Elijah appear with Jesus on the mount. "The first effect of the transfiguration on the apostles," writes one commentator, "was doubtless to convince them beyond any shadow of doubt of the real existence of the other world, the eternal kingdom. Our world is not the only one; there is another."[21]

A second effect of the transfiguration on the disciples is that they understood that other world to be "not just future to our world, but concurrent with it, though also before it and beyond it."[22] Christ had contact with both worlds at the same time. He is transfigured before Peter, James and John, while at the same time He is conversing with Moses and Elijah. It is significant that Moses and Elijah lived in different centuries on earth, but are together with Christ on the mount.

A third lesson from the transfiguration concerns the condition of Moses and Elijah. They are seen in their "glorious splendor" (Luke 9:31). Whether this means that they had already received their glorified bodies (which seems unlikely in light of the teaching of Second Corinthians 5), or that existence in God's presence bestows a pre-resurrection radiance, is difficult to determine. They may have simply and literally "shared His glory." They appear as humans and are engaged in conversation with Jesus. But they are "in glorious splendor."

The most important lesson from the transfiguration concerns the Person of Christ. The transfiguration is not about Moses and Elijah, or about Peter's desire to honor them, or even about our future destiny in glory. The focus is on God's well-beloved Son. *He* is the incarnate God who came to "accomplish [His] departure," specifically at Jerusalem. The subject of conversation between Moses, Elijah and Jesus was not the sweetness of heaven but the sacrifice at Calvary, not the delight of eternity with the saints but His death on a cross for sinners.

We know from Scripture that we will be like Moses and Elijah in our glorified bodies, yet we will still be recognizable as human beings. We will be able to converse with Jesus about what is important, about what is *most* important, for His death and glorious victory over death will be our eternal topic of conversation!

As we get ready for heaven, let us be reminded that heaven indeed has come down to us. And the only reason any of us, from the spiritual giants Elijah and Moses, to the most simple saint of today, can expect to join Jesus in glory is because of His exodus, His sacrifice which He accomplished at Jerusalem. And the conversation about that event will last throughout eternity.

SEVEN

Endless *In*activity?

In a London churchyard, the grave of what must have been an overworked housewife bears this epitaph:

> Weep not for me, friends,
> Though death do us sever,
> I am going to do nothing
> Forever and ever.

(Ripley's Believe It or Not, Ripley International)

"What *are* we born for?" "For infinite happiness," said the Spirit.

(C.S. Lewis)

If I find in myself a desire which no experience in this world can satisfy, the most probable explanation is that I was made for another world.

(C.S. Lewis)

After that, we who are still alive and are left will be caught up together with them in the clouds to meet the Lord in the air. And so we will be with the Lord forever. Therefore encourage each other with these words.

(1 Thessalonians 4:17-18)

*Then I heard every creature in heaven and on earth
and under the earth and on the sea, and all that is in
them, singing: "To him who sits on the throne and to
the Lamb be praise and honor and glory and power,
for ever and ever!" The four living creatures said,
"Amen," and the elders fell down and worshiped.*

(Revelation 5:13-14)

I t was a Sunday morning and the Jones family had just
sung the first few lines of the classic hymn, "Come,
We That Love the Lord":

Come, we that love the Lord,
    And let our joys be known;
Join in a song with sweet accord,
    Join in a song with sweet accord,
And thus surround the throne,
    And thus surround the throne.

David, five years old, looked concerned and whispered
to his mother, "Mom, I don't want to clean in heaven!"

"Whatever do you mean, Dear?" asked his mother.

"Well, we just sang, 'And dust around the throne—and
dust around the throne'! "

Fortunately, the little boy just misunderstood the lyrics;
we won't spend eternity cleaning in heaven! But it does
raise the question: What will we be doing? Some Christians give the impression that we will be having a church
service much like here on earth, but it will go on *forever*.
That is not a happy thought for many of us!

A Few Questions

I happen to like all kinds of music, from Oldies to the Classics (early Beatles is my favorite) to a tape I'm listening to now (it's a collection of Gregorian music, from a group of overweight monks—I think they call themselves "Fat Chants"). What will we *hear* in heaven? What will it sound like? Will there be singing—and if so, will it be music that both we—*and our teenagers*—will like?

I assume I'm not going to need my daily appointment book in heaven. But what will we *do*? Will there be a schedule? We know there will be no night there, and presumably we won't need to sleep. But what will be the activities of the day, I mean, of *eternity*?

The existentialist philosopher Jean-Paul Sartre said that hell is other people. But what about heaven? We won't be alone there. What will our human relations look like? Will we recognize each other? Will we want to?

Will we have anything to do with angels? How about the new heavens and the new earth? Will we be returned to the pristine innocence and beauty of the Garden of Eden before the First Family's rebellion? Are we really going to be taking harp lessons in the clouds?

And what will it be like to see God? Will He be happy to have us there in heaven? Will He be angry with us if we did not serve Him to the best of our abilities? What about rewards or punishments for the Christian? Will there be eternal distinctions which will separate more faithful believers from those who were not as diligent in serving Christ?

We know from First John 3:2 that "when he appears, we shall be like him, for we shall see him as he is." What will it be like to be like Him? Will we be no longer like ourselves?

Our questions continue to multiply. But what do we know *for sure* from Scripture?

Heaven and Self

From our discussion in the previous chapter about the transfiguration, we saw that Moses and Elijah retained their personal identities, even though they were in an after-death condition. They were recognizable to Peter, James and John and were capable of conversation. And yet we are told that they appeared "in glorious splendor" (Luke 9:31).

We are informed in First Corinthians 13:12, "Now we see but a poor reflection as in a mirror; then we shall see face to face. Now I know in part; then I shall know fully, even as I am fully known." This verse seems to say that we will recognize each other, but will we recognize *ourselves*?

New Bodies!

We learn in Second Corinthians 5:1 that we will not be body-less in heaven. Paul teaches us that "we have a building from God, an eternal house in heaven, not built by human hands." We are not destined to live a disembodied existence! (Could it be that the "place" Jesus has gone to prepare for us, as described in John 14:2-3, is our new *bodies*?) At any rate, Paul says that we presently groan in these corruptible, earthly "tents" in which we dwell, that we believers have a "longing to be clothed with our *heavenly dwelling*" (2 Corinthians 5:2).

In contrast to the pre-sin condition of Adam and Eve, the believer has no desire to "be found naked" (5:3). While we are in these earthly bodies (Paul calls our body "this tent"), "we groan and are burdened, because we do not wish to be unclothed but to be clothed with our *heavenly dwelling*, so that what is mortal may be swallowed up by life" (5:4). Although what is "mortal" will be swallowed up by death, death itself (for the believer) will be gobbled up by something much larger—life—God's life!

While we are in these earthly tents, "we groan, being burdened," Paul says (NASB). The Greek word for "groan" here means to "sigh because of an undesirable circumstance."[1] The idea of "being burdened" can also mean "weighed down."[2] Could it be that our earthly bodies are, in a sense, too *heavy* for heaven? The idea of the believer "groaning" is also referred to by Paul in Romans 8:18-23:

> I consider that our present sufferings are not worth comparing with the glory that will be revealed in us. The creation waits in eager expectation for the sons of God to be revealed. For the creation was subjected to frustration, not by its own choice, but by the will of the one who subjected it, in hope that the creation itself will be liberated from its bondage to decay and brought into the glorious freedom of the children of God. We know that the whole creation has been groaning as in the pains of childbirth right up to the present time. Not only so, but we ourselves, who have the firstfruits of the Spirit, groan inwardly as we wait eagerly for our adoption as sons, the redemption of our bodies.

It is not simply the believer who is "groaning"; creation itself "waits in eager expectation" because it "was subjected to frustration." It looks for liberation "from its bondage to decay" and anticipates the day when it will be "brought into the glorious freedom of the children of God." A day of deliverance and of *delivery* will come for creation which has been in labor ("the pains of childbirth") right up to the present time.

Believers are groaning, for we are waiting eagerly for our adoption as sons, specifically for "the redemption of our bodies." Again, C.S. Lewis hits the nail on the head when he speaks about the physical side of our redemption:

> I know some muddle-headed Christians have talked as if Christianity thought that sex, or the body, or pleasure, were bad in themselves. But they were wrong. Christianity is almost the only one of the great religions which thoroughly approves of the body—which believes that matter is good, that God Himself once took on a human body, that some kind of body is going to be given to us even in Heaven and is going to be an essential part of our happiness, our beauty, and our energy. Christianity has glorified marriage more than any other religion: and nearly all the greatest love poetry in the world has been produced by Christians.[3]

In evangelical circles we sometimes speak of someone's "soul being saved"; it is probably more accurate to speak of their total person being saved. The redemption of the body awaits its fulfillment in heaven.

Deposit, Please!

Is that promise of a new body, a "heavenly dwelling," merely a vague hope? No, we are told in Second Corinthians 5:5 that God has given us a *deposit* on that new body: the Holy Spirit! "Now it is God who has made us for this very purpose and has given us the Spirit as *a deposit*, guaranteeing what is to come." Paul also says earlier in the book (1:22) that God has "set his seal of ownership on us, and put his Spirit in our hearts as a deposit, guaranteeing what is to come."

Ephesians 1:13-14 specifies some of what happened to the Christian upon conversion: "Having believed, you were marked in him with a seal, the promised Holy Spirit, who is *a deposit* guaranteeing our inheritance until the redemption of those who are God's possession. . . ." We are commanded, "And do not grieve the Holy Spirit of God, with whom you were sealed for the day of redemption" (4:30). The term "seal" has the idea of a mark of ownership. We *belong* to God; His Holy Spirit is the evidence, the down payment, of our redemption.

In Second Corinthians 5:6-9, Paul launches into his "absent from the body . . . present with the Lord" (KJV) speech. As we saw in our discussion in Chapter 2, Paul visualizes three stages of the believer's existence: (1) an embodied state on this earth in which the believer who is at "home in the body" is "absent from the Lord"; (2) a disembodied state upon death in which the believer's soul or spirit is in the presence of his Savior; and (3) an embodied state in which the believer's soul or spirit is united with his glorified body (which is like Christ's resurrection body [note 1 Corinthians 15]). Although there is no specific statement in the Bible that says that each human being has an immortal soul, passages such as Philippians 1:20-26, Second Corinthians 5:6-10 and Luke 16:19-31 give strong support for belief in a continued existence beyond death for both the believer and the unbeliever. The last passage (Luke 16:19-31, considered in Chapter 2) clearly teaches the after-death existence of both an unbeliever (the rich man) and a believer (Lazarus).

Let's take a closer look at those verses in Second Corinthians 5.

A Confusing Confidence

Paul makes a rather strange comment in verse 6: "Therefore we are always confident and know that as long as we are at home in the body we are away from the Lord." What does he mean by those words? How does the believer's present separation from the Lord inspire confidence? His answer appears in the very next verse: "We live by faith, not by sight." The believer's present condition of being separated from the Lord provides the challenge of living by faith in His promises, rather than becoming discouraged by what our earthly eyes see. Our present lack of vision should not lessen our commitment to the truth God has given us.

Paul repeats his confidence in verse 8 when he writes, "We are confident, I say, and would prefer to be away from the body and at home with the Lord." When you get right down to it, Christian, wouldn't *you* prefer to be with the Lord?

My daughter, who is completing her sophomore year of college, has her own unique personality. She analyzes things (her mom would say too much), especially spiritual issues. Often she has said to us after watching the evening news, "I wish I could just be with Jesus. This is such an awful world. Won't heaven be great?!" Her preference would be to see the Lord Jesus in heaven and to "leave this vale of tears." Paul had the same preference. He would have preferred to "be away from the body and at home with the Lord."

More important than our personal preferences, Paul reminds us, is our *present obedience*: "So we make it our goal to please him, whether we are at home in the body or away from it" (5:9). One overarching concern ought to mark our lives, whether we are present in this world (in our bodies) or present with the Lord (in a disembodied state): to please the Lord! The late mystery novelist Harry Kemelman once said, "In this life you sometimes have to choose between pleasing God and pleasing man. In the long run it's better to please God—He's more apt to remember." Paul's prayer for the Colossian Christians was

> that you may live a life worthy of the Lord and may *please* him in every way: bearing fruit in every good work, growing in the knowledge of God, being strengthened with all power according to his glorious might so that you may have great endurance and patience, and joyfully giving thanks to the Father, who has qualified you to share in the inheritance of the saints in the kingdom of light. (Colossians 1:10-12)

The very idea of living in a way that *pleases* the Lord is foreign to many believers. Rather than walking by faith in this life, making choices which honor Him, they seem to slink around with their arms covering their heads, waiting for God's lightning to strike them dead! God wants us to live confident, worthy, pleasing, fruit-bearing, maturing, strong lives that will keep us going in the tough times and give us joy while we're waiting for our eternal inheritance. And it is encouraging to know that *it is possible* to please the Lord. There should be many moments in the Christian's life when he can echo the words of David to the Lord: "I know that *you are pleased with me* . . ." (Psalm 41:11).

Christians Judged?!

The story is told of a skinny little man who stood before St. Peter at the pearly gates. "In order to get into heaven," Peter said, "you have to tell me of some great deed that you did on earth. Have you done anything memorable and brave during your life?"

The man thought for a while and then said, "Yes, St. Peter, I think I've got something I can offer. I was walking down the street one day when I saw a little old lady being mugged by a Hell's Angels motorcycle gang member. I went up to him and told him to leave her alone. He laughed at me, so I punched him in the face!"

"Sir, that's an incredible story!" St. Peter said. "By the way, when did this happen?"

"Oh," said the man, looking at his watch, "about thirty seconds ago!"

Don't expect to be given the third degree by St. Peter when you get to heaven, despite all the apocryphal stories to the contrary. But be forewarned: Christians *will* be evaluated for how they lived their lives. From expressing his longing to be with Christ in Second Corinthians 5, Paul moves to the sobering truth of judgment for the believer. "For we must all appear before the judgment seat of Christ," he teaches, "that each one may receive what is due him for the things done while in the body, whether good or bad" (5:10). The idea that Christians will not experience *any* judgment is a myth.

I used to be a registered baseball umpire when we lived in Canada. I enjoyed working with young people, especially in an area where baseball was a distant second to hockey, the national pastime. Being an umpire, where all my decisions were final, also gave me some perspective on the final judgment. Someone has said, "Most of us are um-pires at heart; we like to call balls and strikes on somebody else."[4] But we Christians will have to give an account for how we individually have played the game of life.

The Bible appears to make a distinction between the Great White Throne judgment (Revelation 20:11-15) and the judgment seat of Christ (2 Corinthians 5:10; cf. 1 Corinthians 3:10-15 and Romans 14:10).[5] The Great White Throne judgment is the event where only unbelievers will appear and the verdict concerns their eternal lostness. At the judgment seat of Christ only believers will appear and the verdict has to do with the rewards they receive for serv-ing the Lord on earth. There are some Christians, however, who understand that there will be one general judgment which is presented in Scripture from different angles.[6]

At any rate, we know that believers will be held responsi-ble for how they lived or failed to live for Christ. The issue is not their salvation, but their faithfulness. We will momen-tarily discuss the issue of rewards in heaven and whether there will be eternal differences between believers.

Heaven and Others

We will be our own selves in glory, but with new bodies. But what about our relationship with others? There are a number of issues to consider here. What does the Bible mean when it says we will "know even as also [we are] known" (1 Corinthians 13:12, KJV)? Does it mean to be *omniscient*? How will we react regarding our loved ones who have not gone to heaven with us?

There are some who claim that no one will miss heaven. The universalist says that all will be saved by God, whether they want to be or not. Universalism is not taught in the Bible, but that has not stopped certain writers from arguing for it anyway. One of the arguments comes from the noted universalist Nels F.S. Ferré. He pulls no punches when he states that

> Some have never really seen how completely contradictory are heaven and hell as eternal realities. Their eyes have never been opened to this truth. If eternal hell is real, love is eternally frustrated and heaven is a place of mourning and concern for the lost. Such joy and such grief cannot go together. There can be no psychiatric split personality for the real lovers of God and surely not for God himself. That is the reason that heaven can be heaven only when it has emptied hell, as surely as love is love and God is God. God cannot be faithless to Himself no matter how faithless we are; and His is the power, the kingdom and the glory.[7]

Ferré says that hell cannot be an "eternal reality" because it would completely contradict his understanding of heaven. It doesn't matter to him that hell is referred to as a place of "everlasting punishment" (Matthew 25:46, KJV), where there is "unquenchable" (3:12) and "eternal" fire (Jude 7), a place described as "outside" the kingdom of God (Matthew 8:12) where the devil, the beast and the false prophet will be "tormented day and night for ever and ever" (Revelation 20:10). Universalists see Jesus' many warnings about hell as merely empty threats. Or worse, they understand Jesus to have been "a man of His times," that is, one who shared the "contradictory and illogical fears and superstitions" of His culture. When the authoritative Word of God is abandoned (as Ferré has done), there remains only one's fallible human reason, and that's a sad foundation upon which to base one's view of eternity!

Will God's love be "eternally frustrated"? No, His plan will be accomplished. Will God eternally weep over those who have spurned His love and rejected His Son? The Bible never teaches that. Those who turn away from Christ will become objects of His wrath (John 3:36; Revelation 11:18).

To say that "heaven can only be heaven when it has emptied hell" is great rhetoric, but where is there even a *shred* of biblical evidence that God will take such action at the end of time? Instead, the Word depicts an eternal *reality* called the lake of fire into which all the unsaved will be cast. Revelation 20:15 says that "the book of life" will be opened on judgment day and "If anyone's name was not found written in the book of life, he was thrown into the lake of fire." A careful study of the fate of the lost shows that *hell* is temporary, but the *lake of fire* is everlasting.

When I was a Bible college student, I remember occasionally getting cards and letters from friends and family members who would write a favorite biblical reference at the bottom of the card or letter which I was supposed to look up. Some would write "John 3:16" or "Proverbs 3:5-6" (this one was particularly appropriate for know-it-all Bible college students). One of my really twisted high school friends would write at the bottom of his letter "Psalm 137:8-9." If you looked up that reference you would discover that it reads: "Happy is he . . . who seizes your infants and dashes them against the rocks." As I said, he was one of my more twisted friends!

An elder in my home church had a favorite reference he would write on his letters: Revelation 20:15 ("If anyone's name was not found written in the book of life, he was thrown into the lake of fire"). At the time I thought it was a strange sentiment; now I know he was expressing his immense gratitude to Christ for saving him from judgment!

The Bible does not teach that all will be saved. And neither should we.[8] What will be our attitude toward those loved ones who died without Christ and will be separated from Him (and us) forever? That is a very difficult question, but we know that God will "wipe away every tear" from the believer in heaven (Revelation 7:17). We will not spend eternity grieving over those who turned away from Christ.

Marriage in Heaven?

What will be our relationship to those we knew on earth *who are with us* in heaven? Will I have a special bond with my wife of over thirty years? Will there be marriage in heaven (à la the Mormons)?

In Matthew 22 Jesus receives a twofold confrontation on the same day. The Pharisees and the Herodians grill Him about paying taxes, then the Sadducees try to embarrass Him with an absurd marital situation, one that seemed like "Peyton Place" applied to theology. The situation brought up by the Sadducees concerned a Mosaic law regarding childbearing, and the woman who could not conceive is married to seven successive (but *unsuccessful*) brothers. The reason for her marrying so many men was to bear a child, but she finally dies as a childless, seven-time widow. The Sadducees' question was, "Whose wife will she be in the resurrection?"

The way the question is framed seems intent on embarrassing Jesus rather than finding out truth about eternity—much like the question, "Can God create a rock heavier than He can lift?" There is no right answer to such an absurd question! (Whether you answer "yes" or "no," the inquirer will retort: "Then there is something that God *cannot do!*" The best response is to say it is a bad question, equivalent to "Have you stopped beating your dog?")

But Jesus is a master at getting to the heart of a matter, and He replies,

> You are in error because you do not know the Scriptures or the power of God. At the resurrection people will neither marry nor be given in marriage; they will be like the angels in heaven. But about the resurrection of the dead—have you not read what God said to you, "I am the God of Abraham, the God of Isaac, and the God of Jacob"? He is not the God of the dead but of the living. (22:29-32)

The issue here is not the need to sort out complicated human relations in eternity. The Sadducees' problem was that they did not even *believe* in immortality. Nor did they care about this poor, barren widow. The comical cruelty of their case study reflected more their cold hearts than a quest for the truth about the afterlife. Jesus soundly rebukes them for their double error. Their failure was a lack of *knowledge:* they knew neither the Scripture nor the power of God. Because the Sadducees were rationalists (they refused to believe in angels or immortality), they did not accept what the Bible implied about the future state.

Rather than navigating through the marital maze which they presented to Jesus, the Lord insists that the *absurdities* of this life will not impinge upon or characterize or complicate that next life. The reason why people will "neither marry nor be given in marriage" is because there is no need for procreation in that next world. This passage should not be used to indicate that earthly marital relationships will have no meaning (or a lesser meaning) in heaven.

Will we recognize each other in heaven? Scripture tells us that we will "know even as also [we are] known" (1 Corinthians 13:12, KJV). We will *truly* know each other in glory, and it will be in a context of absolute love!

The Issue of Rewards

The question of our personal relationships in heaven leads to the question of whether there will be eternal distinctions there based on our faithfulness here. In his article, "Degrees of Rewards in the Kingdom of Heaven," Craig L. Blomberg argues that there is not "a single NT text that, when correctly interpreted, supports the notion that believers will be distinguished one from another for all eternity on the basis of their works as Christians."[9]

Let's look at several of his primary points. Using the parable of the laborers in the vineyard (Matthew 20:1-16), he argues that all true disciples are equal in God's eyes, even though some join the work at a late date. He sees the principle of merit and ability being set aside so that grace can prevail.[10]

> There does seem to be scriptural support for the doctrine of degrees of punishment in hell, according to the extent of one's conscious transgression of God's laws (see esp. Luke 12:47-48; cf. Matthew 10:15; 11:22, 24; cf. also possibly Romans 5:13), but precisely by this very lack of symmetry between works and grace we would not expect endless gradations of reward within heaven.[11]

The biblical teaching on heaven, especially Revelation 21-22, indicates that " 'there will be no more death or mourning or crying or pain'—absolutely nothing to make one sad."[12]

Those who hold that there will be varying rewards for Christians in heaven (such as John MacArthur and J.I. Packer) suggest that some will have a greater capacity for serving God; others will receive added responsibilities. There will be degrees of bliss, argue some writers, a concept that may include an enriched relationship with God.[13] Blomberg, however, rightly questions the logic of this theory: "If the heavenly aspect of eternal life represents perfection, is it not fundamentally self-contradictory to speak of degrees of perfection?"[14]

Blomberg touches on the five passages having to do with believers' crowns (1 Corinthians 9:25; 1 Thessalonians 2:19; 2 Timothy 4:8; James 1:12; 1 Peter 5:4) and discusses First Corinthians 3:10-15, which "clearly distinguishes between the qualities of believers' works and their rewards on judgment day."[15] There are also several texts that identify people who are "least" or "greatest" in the kingdom (Matthew 5:19; 11:11; 18:4; Mark 9:34-35; Luke 9:48).

Concerning the *crowns*, a majority of commentators agree that the five instances are not talking about degrees of reward in heaven but simply about eternal life. First Corinthians 9:25 has to do with a race and competing for the crown "that will last forever." "Paul is not concerned to compare first place with second or third but to contrast finishing the race with not finishing at all. . . . Eternal life and death are at stake here, not gradations of reward," says Blomberg.[16] A misunderstanding of eternal security has led many Christians to doubt that Paul could have seriously considered not "making it to heaven." But "no biblical text offers assurance of salvation for people who flagrantly repudiate Christ without subsequent repentance." Blomberg quotes Anthony Hoekema: "Only as he thus continued to discipline himself did Paul feel justified in claiming his spiritual security in Christ. He did not dare to claim this blessing while being careless and indolent in his daily battle against sin. And neither may we."[17]

The "crown of exultation" (1 Thessalonians 2:19, NASB) is synonymous with the "hope" and "joy" of eternal life itself. The "crown of righteousness" (2 Timothy 4:8) is awaiting all who long for Christ's appearing. (Those who don't wish for Christ's return cannot truly have been his disciples.) The "crown of life" (James 1:12) seems to refer to all who are Christians. The "crown of glory that will never fade away" (1 Peter 5:4) also seems to be a metaphor for eternal life.

The twenty-four elders in Revelation 4:10, who cast their crowns before God's throne, are angelic creatures, Blomberg suggests, rather than raptured believers. Alternatively, the elders may represent the whole church, in which case the passage shows that "whatever differences believers may experience on judgment day are not perpetuated throughout eternity."[18]

First Corinthians 3:10-15 is often cited to prove that some Christians will be more greatly rewarded for their lives of service than others. The passage reads:

> By the grace God has given me, I laid a foundation as an expert builder, and someone else is building on it. But each one should be careful how he builds. For no one can lay any foundation other than the one already laid, which is Jesus Christ. If any man builds

> on this foundation using gold, silver, costly stones, wood, hay or straw, his work will be shown for what it is, because the Day will bring it to light. It will be revealed with fire, and the fire will test the quality of each man's work. If what he has built survives, he will receive his reward. If it is burned up, he will suffer loss; he himself will be saved, but only as one escaping through the flames.

Before we look at Blomberg's discussion of this passage, let's note several key points. There is only one foundation, and that is the work of the Lord Jesus (3:11). Works done in the Christian's life do not bring salvation; that salvation-producing work has already been accomplished by the Son of God. That does not mean, however, that the Christian can sit on his hands and glide to glory. There is a responsibility to *build on* that foundation.

Note also that every believer is a *builder*, whether he wants to be or not! The Christian's challenge is to "be careful how he builds" (3:10). That "care" is not explained in the text, but both the quantity and the quality of the Christian's building may be in view here.

Note also that there is available a variety of building materials for the Christian to use. Paul lists them, we find out later, in an order emphasizing their value and durability: "gold, silver, costly stones, wood, hay or straw" (3:12). The believer is free to choose his materials, although he will give an account for his choice.

A time of inspecting the building will come, and there will be no opportunity to "grease the palm" of the building inspector! The Christian's work "will be shown for what it is" (3:13). What may have appeared to be a sturdy and glamorous building will be shown to be a spiritual shack. The pretense of some believers will collide with the reality of an all-knowing God. The tool He will use to reveal the building's nature is one often connected with *judgment* in the Word of God—fire. Fire is the great purifier—or incinerator! In fact, Paul says there are only two possible outcomes that are "revealed with fire": (1) the survival of what has been built; or, (2) the destruction of what has been built.

The reward for the Christian will come only with regard to that which survives (3:14). We are told that there are consequences if the building is "burned up." The Christian "will suffer loss" (3:15). There will be, it seems, at least a temporary sense of loss in heaven.

Paul quickly points out that if the Christian's building is burned up, this will not mean his loss of salvation. "If it is burned up," Paul writes, "he will suffer loss; he himself will be saved, but only as one escaping through the flames" (3:15). From this text it appears possible, although certainly not desirable, that a genuine believer can enter heaven with nothing to show for his Christian life.

In discussing this passage, Blomberg acknowledges that there does appear to be a "clear distinction between believers whose works endure their fiery purgation and those whose flimsy construction projects are consumed."[19] He also affirms the uniqueness of each believer's personal encounter with Christ on judgment day. But "nothing in the text says anything about these distinctions among believers' experiences persisting for all time." Citing First John 2:28 ("And now, dear children, continue in him, so that when he appears we may be confident and unashamed before him at his coming"), Blomberg remarks that this passage "anticipates [that] some Christians may experience more shame than others when Christ returns, but no Scripture ever suggests that shame remains a component of heavenly life beyond the immediate context of the *parousia* [the Second Coming of Christ]."[20]

Concerning the passages having to do with "least" or "greatest" in the kingdom, Blomberg says these relate to the present, not the future, aspect of the kingdom. Texts that seem to assign a superior place to the twelve apostles perhaps refer to all believers. Blomberg also suggests that the phrase "lay up treasure for themselves as a firm foundation for the coming age" (1 Timothy 6:19) has to be understood in the context of the rest of the verse: "take hold of the life that is truly life." In the same way, the context of "treasure[s] in heaven" (Matthew 6:20; 19:21) shows that it is essentially the same as "get[ting] eternal life" (19:16) and "enter[ing] the kingdom of heaven" (19:23).

Will Christians have to give an account to the Lord for every deed performed (Romans 2:6; Revelation 22:12) and word uttered (Matthew 12:36; Luke 12:2-3)? Yes! However, Blomberg responds,

> . . . nothing in the contexts of any of those passages suggests varying degrees of reward or the perpetuating of distinctions beyond the Day of the Lord. The purpose of Christians' standing before God's bar of justice is to declare them acquitted, not to embarrass them before the entire cosmos for all their failings (Romans 2:7; Revelation 22:14; Matthew 12:37a). The contrast in each of these three passages is between the saved and the lost, not between two or more different kinds of believers.[21]

James and John ask to sit at Christ's right and left hands in Mark 10:35-45. Although His reply in 10:40 perhaps leaves the door open for some people to receive such a higher status, Christ refuses to discuss that option, redirecting his disciples' attention to servanthood instead, says Blomberg.[22] Jesus is not encouraging us to entertain any notion of a "heavenly hierarchy."

He treats the parables of the talents (Matthew 25:14-30) and the pounds (Luke 19:11-27, KJV) as showing a contrast between believers and unbelievers, rather than between believer and believer. To suggest that the "darkness" of Matthew 25:30 which is "outside" and where there is "weeping and gnashing of teeth" as a less desirable compartment of heaven "defies all credulity. Matthew uniformly uses that language to describe hell" (8:12; 13:42, 50; 22:13; 24:51).[23]

Other texts fail to show such a hierarchy. Philippians 3 has Paul pressing on "toward the goal to win the prize for which God has called me heavenward in Christ Jesus" (3:14), but the context shows that the prize is "to attain to the resurrection from the dead" (3:11). "There is no unambiguous NT doctrine of varying eternal rewards for believers."[24]

Blomberg concludes by reminding us that our performance-centered culture, competition, longer work hours, and less job security contrast with the NT manifesto of grace:

> Far too many Christians whom I have personally encountered think that God relates to them just like the taskmasters they have known in their families and at their work. If only they can be a little more obedient today, God will like them more and deal with them more favorably.[25]

If Blomberg's understanding of this issue is correct, then the Christian will see himself not in competition with other believers, but as individually responsible to move ahead in godliness. There will be a day of reckoning—and there will be tears of regret. But they will not be eternal tears.

Heaven and the Rest of Creation

Scripture provides some interesting insights on our glorified bodies and our heavenly relationship to other humans, but what does the Word say about the rest of creation? What will be our relation to angels, for instance? First Corinthians 6:1-4 tells us that we will judge them:

> If any of you has a dispute with another, dare he take it before the ungodly for judgment instead of before the saints? Do you not know that the saints will judge the world? And if you are to judge the world, are you not competent to judge trivial cases? Do you not know that we will judge angels? How much more the things of this life! Therefore, if you have disputes about such matters, appoint as judges even men of little account in the church!

Some think this means we will conduct a "performance review" of the angels' work in helping us on earth. It seems reasonable to me, however, that Paul is referring to *fallen* angels (probably demons). On the other hand, Paul did not intend that we spend a great deal of time speculating about our role in judgment. Rather, he is arguing from the greater to the lesser. Paul is saying, "If at the end of time, Christian, you will be used by God to judge fallen angels, how is it that you can't settle church disputes in this life?"

What About Fido?

It may seem a frivolous question to some, but there are many Christians who ask, "will there be animals in heaven?" A recent book entitled *Will I See Fido in Heaven?*, subtitled *Scripturally Revealing God's Eternal Plan for His Lesser Creatures*, categorically declares that all animals will go to heaven. We believe it important to discuss certain points made in this book.

The author, Mary Buddemeyer-Porter, asked God to reveal to her whether "our four-legged friends" and the rest of the "lesser creatures" will live eternally in heaven, and she believes that God did just that. She says that her work, *Will I See Fido in Heaven?* "is from God and of God, and its truth will bring many to God."[26]

Her study is more than an academic exercise; she literally believes that her coming to understand that animals have eternal life rescued her from atheism. She says, "I was not looking forward to an eternal life because I could not imagine living without the animals I cherished."[27] She found great comfort in the belief that "for all the torture and abuse that many of the innocent animals suffered throughout God's earth, they will be rewarded in Heaven with eternal bliss."[28]

Mrs. Buddemeyer-Porter argues that because the animal world is innocent of Adam and Eve's rebellion against God, animals are born with a "spiritual wisdom" (which humans have to work to attain).[29] She believes that there are "many, many accounts of animals that have demonstrated spiritual knowledge and understanding beyond what the natural man can comprehend."[30] "The spirits of animals and the elect angels have never been separated from God," she states.[31]

Defining the "soul" as "the psyche, the mind, the emotions, the self-image—the psychological being apart from the spiritual being," Mrs. Buddemeyer-Porter declares that "both the lesser animals and man have a soul."[32] Lesser animals do not have the power of choice, however. Defining the "spirit" as "the essence and will of God given to all humans and animals,"[33] she states, "Remember, the animals also have a spirit from God, and because they are sinless, they have remained attached to God. Although we can know the soul of man and animals, we cannot know the spirit of either."[34]

Believing that "Jesus sacrificed His life on the cross so all God's creatures could have eternal life,"[35] she suggests that "animals . . . too, can be redeemed."[36] She also states that ". . . the animals await Jesus' return along with Christians"[37] and will receive brand-new resurrection bodies at the end of time. She quotes Paul's words: "Who shall change our vile body, that it may be fashioned like unto his glorious body, according to the working whereby he is able even to subdue all things unto himself." (Philippians 3:21, KJV).[38] She insists that "animals forgive and are at peace with the world."[39] Concerning the repentance in the book of Jonah, she writes: "These sinful people are repenting, and even the animals have to dress up and fast to help get out of another one of man's messes."[40]

Some Concerns

I must say that I identified with much of Mrs. Buddemeyer-Porter's concerns about our treatment of the animal world. Although she does not advocate vegetarianism (based on her reasons, could there be a greater case for such a lifestyle?), her call to respect God's "lesser crea-

tures" is certainly biblical. Her anecdotes of animals showing courage, humor and compassion are heartwarming,
and therein lies one of the dangers.

I have several serious concerns about her book. First, her
use of material outside the Bible needs to be reconsidered.
She believes that "God miraculously made the books of the
Apocrypha from the Catholic Bible available to me," for
"passages from these books not only support the Protestant
Bible, but also add depth to it. They make the message easier
to understand, and add credence concerning the eternal
destination of both man and animals."[41] She accepts an
apocryphal story about the Apostle John and a child's dead
dog as factual.[42] She cites *Sirach* (an apocryphal book) and
Matthew's Gospel in conjunction, implying that they are
equally authoritative.[43] She uses the apocryphal *Book of Wisdom* to support her contention that "[God's] imperishable
spirit is in everything!" (Wisdom 12:1).[44] Mrs. Buddemeyer-
Porter appears unaware of the issues of canonicity (why we
have the books we do in our Bibles).

She also states, "A proper respect for animals is seen in
the Native Americans' custom of thanking God for an animal before killing it, and asking the animal to forgive them
for physically destroying it. We can learn so much from
our Indian neighbors."[45] In using these other sources for
her information, I believe she departs from the Bible and
the Bible alone as the Christian's final authority for life
and doctrine. (Where in the Bible do we find any apologies
for the extensive sacrificial system commanded by God?)

Several minor criticisms might include the fact that she
suggests that the fall of man made all living things "worth-
less."[46] I believe the term she really means is "unworthy."
Concerning Adam and Eve's rebellion in the Garden, she

states, "After man disobeyed God and fell into sin, God had to keep man from living forever in his physical state."[47] Doesn't she mean *sinful* state? When she argues for the *sinlessness* of animals,[48] I believe she misunderstands Romans 8:20-21. Those verses do not state that animals are sinless, but say, "For the creation was subjected to frustration, not by its own choice, but by the will of the one who subjected it, in hope that the creation itself will be liberated from its bondage to decay and brought into the glorious freedom of the children of God." It seems that Mrs. Buddemeyer-Porter has missed the Scripture's use of *personification*, a technique which gives human qualities either to inanimate objects or to the animal world to make a point. Some examples of personification would include singing mountains and clapping trees (Isaiah 55:12), shouting valleys (Psalm 65:13), joyfully clapping rivers (98:8), mocking cedars of Lebanon (Isaiah 14:8), "wise" animals (Proverbs 30:24-28), etc.

She also seems to misunderstand First Peter 1:19 in its reference to Christ "as of a lamb without blemish and without spot" (KJV) when she argues that animals are innocent and sinless and "will have immortal life."[49] If "the free will given to man is a distinct factor that separates us from the lesser creatures,"[50] how can a creature without *choice* be declared *sinless*? And yet she insists, "Animals are in tune and at peace with nature, with God."[51] If animals do not have free choice, then how are we to understand her belief that, like Native Americans, we should ask an animal's forgiveness before we kill it?[52]

I also believe she errs when she says, "There is no sin that God cannot forgive and forget."[53] Perhaps *she* has forgotten the passages having to do with the "unpardonable" or "unforgivable" sin (Matthew 12:31-32; Mark 3:28-29).

My greatest concern has to do with Mrs. Buddemeyer-Porter's failure to distinguish between human beings *made in the image of God* and the animal world. She writes, "It seems selfish that we of the human race think that of all creation, we should be the only creatures of any eternal importance."[54] According to her work, the human being has a *soul*, but the *animal* also has a soul. The human being has a *spirit*, but the *animal* also has a spirit. She does say that mankind has the power of choice (which animals don't), but that seems to be a negative quality, rather than something which makes us unique and reflective of our status as image-bearers of God. Animals in her understanding actually appear to have a superior *spiritual status* to man. She writes,

> The spirits of the animals remained connected with God [after man's rebellion in the Garden], though, allowing them to see beyond the temporal state, which they were forced to live in because of man's sin. Man, however, became trapped in the temporal state of this life because of his spiritual separation from God.[55]

A Critical Definition

What does it mean, then, to have "eternal" or "everlasting" life? She never really defines the term biblically. Although we will focus on that expression in our last chapter, we must point out here that Jesus defines "eternal life" as follows:

> Father, the time has come. Glorify your Son, that your Son may glorify you. For you granted him au-

> thority over all *people* that he might give *eternal life*
> to all those you have given him. Now this is *eternal*
> *life*: that they may *know you*, the only true God, and
> *Jesus Christ*, whom you have sent. (John 17:1-3)

Eternal life is a *personal relationship* with the Father and the
Son. Only *persons* can have *personal relationships*, despite the
fact that all of us (including myself) carry on conversations
with our pets! Although she says, "I realize that I must be
very clear about man's relationship to eternal life,"[56] she fails
to include in her glossary such critical terms as "eternal life,"
"image of God," "soul" or "spirit."

I appreciate her concern that we should exercise a godly
dominion over this world, but I believe she has paid too high
a price for making that point: she has gone beyond the authority and teaching of the Bible, the Word of God; she has
blurred the distinction between the human being made in
the image and likeness of God and the animal world; and she
has misunderstood "eternal life" as longevity of existence
(rather than a personal relationship with the Creator).

Will there be animals in heaven? I don't see the Bible ad-
dressing this issue as specifically as Mrs. Buddemeyer-Porter
desires. However, I appreciate her comment that the more
important question is, "Will Fido see *you* in heaven?" Our focus should be on human beings who need the gospel, while
we treat God's creation with respect. Beyond that, we can
trust Him to do what is right. I think my dog will be in glory,
but I don't have any Bible verses to support my opinion.

Heaven and God

There is a direct correlation between our longing for
heaven and our understanding of the Person of God. Not

surprisingly, those who don't believe the gospel prefer not to believe in God either. "For my own part," the skeptic Julian Huxley once admitted, "the sense of spiritual relief which comes from rejecting the idea of God as a supernatural being is enormous."[57] But rejecting the *idea* of God provides a fast, but false, relief.

If we hold a poor view of God, we will undoubtedly shrink away from the biblical teaching that the primary reason for "going to heaven" is to be with our Creator, our Savior, our Best Friend. One should not be surprised that much effort has gone into describing the atmosphere, citizens, activities, surroundings, and beauties of heaven, rather than its central attraction—God Himself! Our concepts of heaven are puny because our concepts of God are so small. If we could imagine the most perfect of all beings, One who is free of any sin, blemish, impurity or deficiency, we would be well on our way, at least, to *beginning* to develop a biblical concept of God.

Part of our difficulty is that we cannot step outside our own tainted minds and conceive of such perfection. And it sometimes strikes us, if we are honest, as somewhat egotistical that God demands His creatures' absolute worship, allegiance—and very lives! We resent human dictators who hold such lofty views of themselves and their regimes. When we conceive of the God of the Bible as that kind of potentate, only infinitely larger, we very well may cringe at the idea that we will worship Him throughout all eternity—and in fact, were created to do so!

The problem is not in God and certainly not in His demands, which are universally *right* and in harmony with all creation. The problem is with *us*—with our pathetic, emaciated views of the Sovereign Creator and Sustainer of all that is, apart from sin.

When we read the following words in Jeremiah 9:23-24, we need to analyze them in order to perform major surgery on our diseased concepts of the Almighty:

> This is what the LORD says:
> "Let not the wise man boast of his wisdom
>   or the strong man boast of his strength
>   or the rich man boast of his riches,
> but let him who boasts boast about this:
>   that he understands and knows me,
> that I am the LORD, who exercises kindness,
>   justice and righteousness on earth,
>   for in these I delight," declares the LORD.

God delights in His own attributes because His attributes are perfect! We spend so much time with our eyes on ourselves that we don't really get to know the characteristics of our perfect God.

The Apostle Paul challenges the believer to "set your hearts on things above, where Christ is seated at the right hand of God" (Colossians 3:1). Our problem is, perhaps, a problem of focus. We need our minds *set*. Have you ever noticed how many people have a VCR which constantly flashes "12:00 . . . 12:00 . . . 12:00"? No one has set the clock; it's obvious to everyone. It is just as obvious that our minds are often focused on many other things than our God.

And when we focus on God, it is important that we look at all that the Bible says about Him and His attributes. We dare not overlook any of the biblical descriptions of God, or our view of Him will be lopsided and uneven. When universalists, for example, quote "God is love" (1 John 4:8, 16) and conclude that therefore *no one can ultimately be lost*, they commit the error of defining God by only one of His attributes. If the biblical statement "our God is a consuming fire" (Hebrews 12:29) were the only description of God in the Bible, we could conclude that He will destroy all things at the end of time, including His blood-bought children!

Although we need to learn all God's attributes as revealed in Scripture to have a well-developed understanding of who God is, that does not mean that some attributes do not merit greater attention. Each generation of Christians has tended to overemphasize some aspect of God's Person, overlook some biblical description of God's character, or reinterpret some character trait for the sake of placating the "spirit of the age." His attributes need to be related to each other so that they will be correctly defined and understood.

I heartily agree with Jonathan Edwards in his statement that "a true love of God must begin with a delight in His holiness, and not with a delight in any other attribute; for no other attribute is truly lovely without this."[58] It should not surprise us that this same scholar preached the classic soul-disturbing sermon "Sinners in the Hands of an Angry God." In our definition-deficient society where "love" means anything from a sexual encounter to a deep affection for one's new motorcycle, we need the Word of God as our glossary.

What will it be like to be in the presence of Someone who is absolutely pure? We will find out in heaven. What will it be like to be in fellowship with the One the Psalmist says "will fill me with joy in your presence, with eternal pleasures at your right hand" (Psalm 16:11)? We will find out in heaven. What will it be like to be forever with the One "in [whom] there is no darkness at all" (1 John 1:5)? We will find out in heaven. But we can make preparations for that meeting right now.

Again, it is C.S. Lewis who has understood the crux of the matter: "God is the only comfort, He is also the supreme terror. . . . Some people talk as if meeting the gaze of absolute goodness would be fun. They need to think again. They are only playing with religion."[59] Only the imputed righteousness of Christ can prepare—and protect—a human being at that encounter.

What will it be like to be with the One in whose image we are made? Occasionally one hears stories of those who have located their birth parents after being given up for adoption many years ago. Sometimes those reunions are disappointing. What must it be like for one that goes well? The realization that one's habits, mannerisms, and very appearance are immediately recognized in the father or mother one has not seen for many years must be incredible. If we are made in His image, will we not respond to Him with a familiarity that will stir us to our very souls? And to know that He did not give us up to be adopted by another, but has Himself waited for this glorious reunion?

Perhaps we need to better understand the truth of God's *greatness*. James Sire argues that

> . . . the greatness of God is the central tenet of Christian theism. When a person recognizes this and consciously accepts and acts on it, this central conception is the rock, the transcendent reference point, that gives life meaning and makes the joys and sorrows of daily existence on planet earth significant moments in an unfolding drama in

which one expects to participate forever, not always with sorrows but someday with joy alone.[60]

When we see the Lord face to face, it will not be as
stranger to stranger. He knows us *perfectly*—and the more
of Him we learn to worship this side of eternity the more
prepared we will be for that meeting. Although we presently walk by faith and not by sight, we can nonetheless
grow in our understanding of the depth of God's love
(Ephesians 1:17; 3:14-19). How sad on that day for those
Christians who did not pursue a closer walk with the Lord.

The Issue of Intimacy

Does it not make sense that if we do not grow closer to the
Lord in *this* life, we will not be as prepared as we could be for
that *next* life? This point is made powerfully by Cynthia
Heald: "God does not have a secret society of intimate
friends. We are as intimate with God as *we* choose to be. It is
our desire, *our* abiding, *our* purity that will determine the
depth of our intimacy with Him."[61] We are talking about an
issue of *choice*. We can choose to grow in our relationship to
God through attention to the Scriptures, a commitment to
biblical prayer (including the much-neglected aspect of adoration), and the discipline of meditating upon His truth.

The difficulty for many of us is that we tend to settle for
what I call "minimalist Christianity." We are glad to be
saved, happy to know we are on our way to heaven, and
marginally committed to the work of the kingdom. But
that's about as far as it goes.

I recently had to move a cargo van filled with my
in-laws' furniture from New Jersey to South Carolina. My
trusty dog Dixie, a gentle Lhasa-Apso/Shih-Tzu combina-

tion, made the twelve-hour trip with me—just the two of us. We did not discuss theology or the writing of this book or classical music or anything during the journey. In fact, Dixie was perfectly happy to sleep the whole way *if* I shared my food with her whenever I stopped for a break. She did tell me, however (though not in so many words, of course!), that she suspects she is addicted to potato wedges.

Now that I think about it, my dog *did* teach me some theology. Is it not true that many of us do not choose to advance in our knowledge of the Lord, but virtually sleep through our journey in life, addicted to this world's "potato wedges"?

First John 3:2 tells us that we "shall see [Christ] as he is." Will it be a completely unexpected encounter, or an occasion of utmost familiarity? Many Americans know that Buzz Aldrin and Neil Armstrong were the first men to set foot on the moon. What many may not be aware of is that Aldrin later suffered an emotional breakdown, followed by a slow, painful recovery. One interviewer asked the astronaut what caused his crisis, and got this response:

> Aldrin said it resulted from the terrible disillusionment he felt after working so hard, achieving every goal set before him, and then finding it empty when it was over. His dreams, fantastic though they were, were not lasting enough. After accomplishing that great goal in his life—walking on the moon—he was left with no purpose or meaning.[62]

Aldrin's problem was that his goal, as lofty as it was, was too small and shortsighted. It was only the moon! What

greater goal could one have for his life than to see the face
of his Creator?

EIGHT

For Heaven's Sake!

We do not wish to build fences around God's grace
... and we do not preclude the possibility that some
in hell might finally be translated into heaven.

(Donald Bloesch)

I find it impossible to avoid offending guilty men,
for there is no way of avoiding it but by our silence
or their patience; and silent we cannot be because
of God's command, and patient they cannot be
because of their guilt.

(Martin Luther)

*Then the King will say to those on his right, "Come,
you who are blessed by my Father; take your inheritance, the kingdom prepared for you since the creation
of the world." ... Then he will say to those on his left,
"Depart from me, you who are cursed, into the eternal
fire prepared for the devil and his angels."*

(Matthew 25:34, 41)

*Knowing therefore the terror of the Lord, we persuade
men.*

(2 Corinthians 5:11, KJV)

I'm afraid I have bad news, Mr. Smith," said a doctor to his patient. "You don't have long to live."

"Really?" said the patient. "How long?"

"Ten," said the doctor.

"Ten?" asked the patient. "TEN? Ten *what?* Ten months? Ten weeks? *What?*"

The doctor responded, "Nine, eight, seven, six . . ."

In this chapter we will look at two major steps the Christian can take, "for heaven's sake," to get ready for glory. The first concerns evangelism; the second concerns sanctification (becoming more like Christ).

It is reported that when the celebrated actor John Barrymore was on his deathbed in 1942, his last words were, "Die? I should say not, dear fellow. No Barrymore would allow such a conventional thing to happen to him."[1] Well, it did happen to him, with or without his approval.

And it will happen to all of us (unless the Second Coming preempts it). Death is the great leveler of all men.

In 1999 "Dr. Death," Jack Kevorkian, who assisted in the suicides of 130 people, stood before Judge Jessica Cooper. He was on trial for injecting Thomas Youk, age fifty-two, with a lethal dose of chemicals in September of 1998 at Youk's request. Judge Cooper expressed misgivings about Dr. Kevorkian's serving as his own attorney. Her question to him was to the point: "Do you understand you could spend the rest of your life in prison?" Kevorkian's response was just as succinct: "There's not much of it left."[2]

We read in the book of James that our lives are "a mist that appears for a little while and then vanishes" (James 4:14). While I am repulsed at Kevorkian's actions, I think everyone should adopt his perspective: "there's not much of it left." Let's take a look at John's Gospel to discover what Jesus, the Incarnate Son of God, said about both death and eternal life.

The Disaster of Death

Traditionally Christians have taught that judgment awaits all who die without a saving knowledge of Jesus Christ. The evangelist Billy Sunday once said, "If there is no hell, a good many preachers are obtaining money under false pretenses." Jesus taught much about what would happen to those who die unprepared to meet God (in fact, *He* is our primary source of information on precisely that issue).[3]

For example, He says in John 8, "I am going away, and you will look for me, and you will *die* in your sin. Where I go, you cannot come" (John 8:21). What is it, precisely, that keeps a person from going to heaven? It is *unbelief* in Christ. Several verses later Jesus says, "I told you that you would *die in your sins*; if you do not believe that I am the one I claim to be, you will indeed *die in your sins*" (John 8:24).

There are some who suggest that death is not as final as John 8:24 implies. For example, the theologian John Sanders says that we should not view death as "the decisive barrier of time for people to make a decision of faith."[4] Contrary to those who suggest that death does not end all opportunities for salvation, Jesus indicates that it does.

To match His incredible claims, Jesus makes an incredible promise: "I tell you the truth, if anyone keeps my word, he will never see death" (John 8:51). This promise is very similar to that made by Jesus in Matthew 16:28 where He says, "some who are standing here will not taste death before they see the Son of Man coming in his kingdom." Both of these verses have Jesus using a double negative in Greek which underscores the absolute impossibility of the believer in Christ "see[ing] death" (John 8:51) on the one hand, and, concerning the three disciples on the mount of transfiguration, the absolute certainty of their not tasting death before they saw the Son of Man coming in His kingdom (Matthew 16:28), as we discussed in Chapter 6.

Allowing a Friend to Die

In John 11, Jesus is informed that His good friend Lazarus is sick. The Lord tells His disciples that "this sickness will not end in death. No, it is for God's glory so that God's Son may be glorified through it" (11:4). Jesus, it appears, purposely stayed away for two more days *in order to give Lazarus time to die*.

Finally He says to His disciples: "Our friend Lazarus *has fallen asleep*; but I am going there to wake him up" (11:11). "Sleep" is sometimes used as a euphemism (a gentler substitute expression) for death, especially the death of a believer (see, for example, Acts 7:60). But Jesus' disciples weren't into euphemisms, so they responded, "Lord, if he sleeps, he will get better" (John 11:12). I can even imagine some of them suggesting home remedies for Lazarus, such as their mothers' chicken soup!

Jesus has to abandon His use of gentle language and declares plainly to them, "Lazarus is *dead*" (11:14). He then adds an ironic note of *gladness*, "and for your sake *I am glad I was not there*, so that you may believe" (11:15). What could be more important than God's protecting His children from physical death? If the death of a believer can be used by God to further the faith of others, *that* is more important than God's rescuing His children from what appears to us to be the ultimate tragedy of this life.

And we know "the rest of the story." Jesus gloriously raises Lazarus from the dead and, as a result, "many of the Jews . . . put their faith in him" (11:45).

But wait a minute! Had not Jesus said, "This sickness will not end in death" (11:4)? He either meant something special by the words "end in," or He must have been talking about a different kind of *death*, for Lazarus *did* die! "Jesus said to her [Martha], 'I am the resurrection and the life. He who believes in me will live, even though he dies; and whoever lives and believes in me will never die. Do you believe this?'" (11:25-26). A paradoxical statement, to be sure. How can one both "live" and "die" at the same time? The interpretation of this would seem to be that belief in Jesus transcends physical death and rescues one from eternal death. He must mean at least two things by the term "die" here. The final result or outcome of this experience in Lazarus' life was not the irreversible condition of being separated from his physical body. At any rate, glory is brought to the Father and the Son through this tragedy (11:4, 40).

Modern Minimizations of Death

Some today use mockery to minimize the prospect of death. The comedian and movie director Woody Allen once said, "Death should not be seen as the end but as a very effective way to cut down expenses." The author W. Somerset Maugham quipped, "Death is a very dull, dreary affair, and my advice to you is to have nothing whatsoever to do with it." Making jokes about death is one way modern men and women cope with their eventual demise.

Others seek longevity. But efforts at postponing death have fallen upon hard times. The average life expectancy at birth has nearly doubled (from forty to seventy-five years) from the mid-nineteenth century. But, as one writer puts it, "there seems to be a kind of biological limit programmed into the cells of the human body. In laboratory experiments, human cells divide only about fifty times before they begin to fall apart like old jalopies."[5] When asked about Methuselah, the grandfather of Noah, who is reported in the Bible to have lived 969 years, a researcher responded, "Someone misplaced a decimal point."[6]

Time magazine interviewed Jeanne Calment of Arles, France, who reached the age of 120 before passing away. When asked the secret of her longevity, she responded, "I took pleasure when I could. I acted clearly and morally and without regret. I'm very lucky."[7]

Some choose not to leave their longevity to luck. It is reported that Walt Disney's body is being preserved through cryonics, the process of freezing a human body in hopes of someday resuscitating and treating the person when medical science finds a cure for the disease that took his life.

Still others treat death as a positive stimulus to productivity and proper behavior in this life. Pico Iyer concludes his *Time* article entitled "Death Be Not a Stranger" by expressing his belief that "thinking about death is useful only if it makes us concentrate on life. . . . The otherworld is relevant only in the shadow it casts on this one."[8]

The Answer Lady

Marilyn vos Savant is a member of Mensa (an exclusive club for those with extra-high intelligence) and is listed by the Guinness Book of World Records as having the world's highest IQ. In her regular column in *Parade* magazine, she was asked by an emergency-room nurse how she thinks about her own eventual death. Her answer is important, for it reflects the contemporary attitude of many toward death:

> I never think about death unless I need to remind myself to enjoy life as much as possible now. This comes in especially handy when I'm searching for a good excuse to do something that I really want to do anyway. But living with the subconscious thought of impending mortality can give life an inspirational or even philosophical edge too. And there's nothing wrong with that, especially if you're an artist or a writer. For most of us, though, I think thoughts of our eventual expiration dates are a big waste of time.[9]

How could someone so smart be so dumb? She never thinks about death unless she needs to remind herself "to enjoy life as much as possible now"? What about *eternity*? Is the only value of thinking about our "impending mortality" the "inspirational or even philosophical edge" it gives us in *this life*? Is it only artists and writers who need that "edge"?

I do not know Ms. vos Savant's religious convictions, but it sounds like she's put all her eggs in the basket of *this* life—and that reminds us of a story told by none other than the Lord Jesus Christ.

A Foolish Farmer

In Luke 12 Jesus gives the parable of a very astute farmer who was blessed with especially fertile land. Recognizing his land's future potential, this businessman analyzed the situation and concluded (quite reasonably) that tomorrow's success depended upon today's planning. If there had been a plaque on this man's desk, it would have read: "If you fail to plan, you are planning to fail!"

Since his primary problem was one of storage, he made a proactive, economic decision: he decided to tear down his present barns in order to make room for bigger ones to hold the grain which would be produced. He was not going to tear down his present barns simply to be destructive. He had an action plan—and that plan revolved around prosperity, abundance and the continuing production of his farm property.

There is no note of censure for what the man was going to do with his property; his error lay in what he did not consider *God* might do with *His* creature's life! That the man had forgotten God becomes clear in Luke 12:19 where he says, "And I will say to my soul [this man even plans what he's going to say to *himself*!], Soul, thou hast much goods laid up for many years; take thine ease, eat, drink, and be merry" (KJV). Whether this man even recognized the existence (much less the need) of his soul is questionable. The word "soul" here may simply be translated "self."

As he anticipates what he is going to say to himself, he makes several value judgments. He finds joy in his "much goods." But how "much goods" does one need to be truly joyful? The multimillionaire John D. Rockefeller was asked the question, "How much money does a man need to be truly happy?" And his reply was, "Just a little bit *more*." This farmer anticipates that these "much goods" would be "laid up for many years." How many? What if the grain market took a nosedive? What if a famine came or he was robbed? What if his own existence on earth came to an abrupt end?

But the real nature of this man's heart is exposed in his conclusion. He envisions his material abundance, calculates a lengthy time period of no worries, and says to himself, "take thine ease, eat, drink, and be merry." Can you picture all the Club Med brochures laid out on his coffee table? He's probably placed an order for a top-of-the-line recliner for his living room, purchased an expensive entertainment center, and signed up for several long-term book-of-the-month clubs! The text is not teaching that comfort is wrong or that a man should not be rewarded for his labor and long-range planning. But this man's "ease" or joy depended solely on his earthly possessions and his human calculations of his continuing existence on earth.

He had left out a major factor in his strategizing: He had overlooked eternity. And before the man can turn his plans into reality, he hears the voice of God. There are no wasted words in God's message to this shortsighted and thoroughly unprepared farmer: "Thou fool, this night thy soul shall be required of thee; then whose shall those things be, which thou hast provided?" (12:20, KJV). He is a prime example, someone has said, of the dictum: "You can't take it with you—but *it* can take *you* with *it*!"

The man may have had some control over his farmland. He may have had some ability to predict the future. But he could not control the mind or purposes of God. He was completely *unprepared* for that final, irreversible, divine interruption of his earthly life. Someone has written about a man who sounds much like our unprepared farmer in Luke 12:

> He wore his boots when it rained. He brushed his teeth twice a day with a nationally advertised toothpaste. The doctors examined him twice a year. He slept with the windows open. He stuck to a diet with plenty of fresh vegetables. He relin-

quished his tonsils and traded in several worn-out
glands. He golfed—but never more than eighteen
holes at a time. He got at least eight hours' sleep
every night. He never smoked, drank or lost his
temper. He did his "daily dozen" daily. He was all
set to live to be a hundred. The funeral will be
held Wednesday. He's survived by eight special-
ists, three health institutions, two gymnasiums,
and numerous manufacturers of health foods and
antiseptics. There was nothing wrong with the
things he did, but they did not prepare him for
death. He made one mistake. He forgot God. And
now he is in hell.

In figuring out his land's future potential, the farmer had
overlooked his own future punishment. His present vision
had been incredibly myopic: He saw only his land and his
wealth and his comfort. He was blind to his soul and to eternity. His greatest need was not to tear down his old barns. It
was that God would tear down his self-reliance and stubborn
this-worldly orientation that left him completely unprepared
for his death. When it came to putting something away for
the *future*, he learned that he had not laid up any real treasures for himself in heaven (12:21) and therefore was not
"rich toward God." And that is reality's deepest and most
profound poverty.

Even Mensa Members Need to Think!

After looking at that foolish farmer, I am reminded
again of that foolish member of Mensa, Marilyn vos Savant. If thoughts of one's own impending demise fail to focus one's attention on that next life, *what will*? Despite the

warnings of Jesus, vos Savant insists that "thoughts of our eventual expiration dates are a big waste of time." It sounds like a bold declaration, but it stands in direct contradiction to the many warnings of Scripture to make sure one is right with God *before* one's expiration date comes!

It may be that Marilyn vos Savant needs to consider Jeremiah's challenge in Jeremiah 9, which we briefly considered in Chapter 7:

> This is what the LORD says:

> "Let not the wise man [or woman] boast of his [or
>   her] wisdom
>   or the strong man boast of his strength
>   or the rich man boast of his riches,
> but let him who boasts boast about this:
>   that he understands and knows me,
> that I am the LORD, who exercises kindness,
>   justice and righteousness on earth,
>   for in these I delight," declares the LORD.
>   (9:23-24)

I certainly do not know Ms. vos Savant's heart, but her attitude toward her "expiration date" may indicate she puts more confidence in her wisdom than in God's Word and its warnings.

When comedian W.C. Fields, a lifelong agnostic, was on his deathbed, a friend found him busily thumbing through a Bible. "Bill," his friend said in surprise, "what are *you* doing reading the Bible?" Fields replied, "I'm looking for a loophole!" There are no loopholes which allow anyone to escape from physical death.

James Matthew Barrie (1860-1937), the Scottish dramatist and novelist who wrote *Peter Pan*, has his main character say, "To die will be an awfully big adventure." The writer James Thurber asked, "But what is all this fear of and opposition to oblivion? What is the matter with the soft darkness, the dreamless sleep?"

Should death be something *fearful*? Yes! For those who do not know Christ death should be feared for its *finality*! Rather than death being an "awfully big adventure," it will be the most awful experience a human can ever face. It will not be "the soft darkness, the dreamless sleep." Jesus warns that there will be weeping and gnashing of teeth (Matthew 8:12; 24:51) that will last forever (Revelation 20:10-15).

The French author and filmmaker Jean Cocteau took this approach to his mortality: "Since the day of my birth, my death began its walk. It is walking toward me, without hurrying."[10] What hopeless fatalism! But such despair is not the lot of Christians. Although Jesus does not guarantee to rescue His followers from physical death, He promises them that death will not have the final word. He has removed "the sting of death" by His glorious resurrection (1 Corinthians 15:54-57).

The Imperative of Evangelism

If, indeed, people who do not believe in Christ are in a moment-by-moment peril of dying "in their sins," how is the believer to respond? When we read the words of Jesus in John 3:36 that "Whoever believes in the Son has eternal life, but whoever rejects the Son will not see life, for God's wrath remains on him," do we understand what God expects from us? It is spiritually irresponsible to interpret that verse to imply that only those who have *heard* the gospel and have consciously *rejected it* are lost.

Jesus makes it clear that *all people* are in a lost condition prior to their putting their faith in Him. No one exists in a state of spiritual neutrality. Earlier in John's Gospel Jesus said, "Whoever believes in him [the Son of God] is not condemned, but whoever does not believe *stands condemned already* because he has not believed in the name of God's one and only Son" (3:18). The reason the Christian is to engage in evangelism is that the unbeliever is *presently* "under the wrath of God," in a state of "condemnation."

I recently read about a man by the name of Daniel Earl Bales, Jr. Mr. Bales will soon leave a Colorado prison. But he has a major problem to solve. "I'm dead," he says, "and I'm really concerned about that." Bales escaped from prison in 1987 and eluded capture for nine years. His wife did not hear from him and petitioned for him to be declared legally dead so that she could collect on a life insurance policy. Bales' problem? He is legally dead! He has to figure out how to get a driver's license and a Social Security card so he can get a job. The wife's lawyer said, "We honestly believed he was dead. We went through all sorts of efforts to locate him. The statute was followed completely, and done in good faith. If [he] is dead, that's his problem."[11]

What we don't realize is that we are all "dead men walking" when we are in our sins. And life, *eternal life*, becomes ours only as someone shares the gospel with us and we believe in Jesus Christ. We are to be wise in our witness, yet we must be convinced that outside of a personal, saving knowledge of Jesus Christ, every person we meet is *lost* and presently under the *wrath of God*. The late theologian Francis Schaeffer sought to stir the church to evangelism when he said that to a great extent evangelical Christians have "lost sense of the lostness of the lost."

If I am a sold-out servant of Jesus Christ, I will be getting ready for heaven by reaching the lost. As a former "dead man walking," I will pray for and seek to communicate the gospel to those who are dead in trespasses and sins (Ephesians 2:1-5, KJV).

Death's Only Remedy: Eternal Life

But Jesus did not speak only of death and its consequences. He often presented the remedy for man's sins, the solution to man's condemnation. Let's notice how often He spoke of "eternal life."

It is from no one other than the Second Person of the Trinity that we hear the words, "For God so loved the world that he gave his one and only Son, that whoever believes in him shall not perish but have *eternal life*" (John 3:16). Almost all preachers take on that famous text, and it's been my experience that when they get to the "so" of John 3:16, they spread their arms out wide to indicate the greatness, the magnificence, of God's love.

The only problem is that the Greek word for "so" does not mean the largeness or quantity of the love of God, but "in the following manner" or "thusly." The verse is focusing upon the *means* by which God showed His love for the world: He gave His only Son. He loved the world "in the following way"—He provided His only Son for the sins of the world. Rather than indicating the *quantity* of God's love (certainly taught in other passages, such as Ephesians 3:14-19), John 3:16 emphasizes the *quality* or *manner* of His care for the world of lost men and women.

John the Gospel writer comments in the same chapter, "Whoever believes in the Son has *eternal life*, but whoever rejects the Son will not see life, for God's wrath remains on him" (John 3:36). A master of metaphor, Jesus illustrates salvation in a fashion abundantly clear to those living in an arid land: ". . . whoever drinks the water I give him will never thirst. Indeed, the water I give him will become in him a spring of water welling up to *eternal life*" (4:14). This may well have been a reference to the Holy Spirit who is the "down payment" of our salvation. Jesus says in John 7:38, "He that believeth on me, as the scripture hath said, out of his belly shall flow rivers of living water" (KJV). John the Gospel writer then provides a divine interpretation for us: "But this spake he of the Spirit, which they that believe on him should receive: for the Holy Ghost was not yet given; because that Jesus was not yet glorified" (7:39, KJV).

Crossing Over the Border

One of my favorite expressions of Jesus' concerning eternal life is that found in John 5:24: "I tell you the truth, whoever hears my word and believes him who sent me has *eternal life* and will not be condemned; he has crossed over from death to life."

My family and I lived in Canada for nine years. Occasionally we would take a trip south to Grand Forks, North Dakota. At the border into the United States, we had to produce our passports for the border guard. I think most of them hated their job; they always seemed to be negative and condescending to Canadian visitors (even though, it seemed, most of the economy of Grand Forks was underwritten by Canadians!).

What really bugged me was the fact that we were American *citizens*! We were not foreigners who needed to be scrutinized, interrogated or mistreated by those customs agents (although Canadians shouldn't be treated that way, either). When I showed them my American passport, I was often tempted to say, "Listen, Mr. Surly Border Guard, I am *an American*—and I have every right to come *back home* to the States—*anytime I want to*, in fact! My passport *guarantees me* that right! Now go pick on somebody else!"

I'm glad I never succumbed to that temptation, for we heard horror stories of how ticked off border guards would virtually dismantle a visitor's automobile, presumably looking for contraband. But you need to know that I was sorely tempted!

Isn't it great to know that whoever hears Jesus' word and believes in Him has eternal life and has crossed over from death to life? *He* is our passport, and He welcomes all who repent and believe to cross over that border of spiritual death.

Jesus and Bible Thumpers

The Pharisees thought they knew the Old Testament perfectly. But Jesus attacks the Bible thumpers of His day when He says: "You diligently study the Scriptures because you think that by them you possess *eternal life*. These are the Scriptures that testify about me, yet you refuse to come to *me* to have life." (John 5:39-40). Knowledge of the Bible is not eternal life! I've engaged in many discussions with Jehovah's Witnesses who "knew their Bibles" (at least, their *New World* translation). But because they did not believe in the real Jesus (according to their theology, Jesus was originally Michael the archangel who gave up his angelic nature so that he could die on a torture stake for mankind and then resurrect spiritually, not bodily), they were not saved. Only the *real* Jesus saves. A Jesus of our own, or others', creation can only delude, mislead and condemn us.

Better Than Sliced Bread

As we continue our survey of John's Gospel, chapter 6 describes the miracle of the feeding of the five thousand and sets forth Christ as the "bread of life." Jesus challenges His disciples: "Do not work for food that spoils, but for food that endures to *eternal life*, which the Son of Man will give you. On him God the Father has placed his seal of approval" (6:27). Later He says, "For the bread of God is he who comes down from heaven and gives *life* to the world" (6:33). Jesus could speak authoritatively of the Father's plan: "For my Father's will is that everyone who looks to the Son and believes in him shall have *eternal life*, and I will raise him up at the last day" (6:40).

Eternal life is a gift from God (6:27), and the biblical reality is that in order for anyone to have *eternal life*, the Son of God had to die. He did not die as a courageous martyr or as the world's most supreme example of goodness. He died as our *sacrifice* (6:33). His blood was shed so that our sins could be forgiven. The natural man or woman does not like the idea that his or her sins necessitated the cruel death of the Son of God on a Roman cross. Delores Williams, Paul Tillich Professor of Theology and Culture at Union Theological Seminary, says, "I don't think we need folks hanging on crosses and blood dripping and weird stuff . . . we don't need atonement, we just need to listen to the god within."[12] But there is no "god within."

The idea of Jesus dying for man's sin is offensive to many. That is one reason why many today believe only what their "heart" tells them to believe. A number of years ago I had an extended conversation with the brother of a friend of mine. This young man had grown up in a Christian home, but had rejected Christianity and was willing to spend time persuading others to do the same. We had some excellent discussions about the evidences for the Christian faith, why Jesus alone is the Savior, the question of other religions, etc. He was particularly enamored with the writings of Joseph Campbell (*The Power of Myth*) and Charles Templeton (*Farewell to God*). When I asked him how he knew what was *true* and worthy of his belief, he said, "Whatever resonates with my heart, whatever stirs my spirit as being true, I *accept as true!*"

I said that he would not like my next comment. Was he sure he wanted to hear it? He said yes, and I replied, "The Bible clearly warns us against trusting our own hearts as to what is ultimately true about God and reality. We read a serious warning about our hearts in Jeremiah 17:9: "The heart is deceitful above all things and beyond cure. Who can understand it?" I then challenged him with the fact that his heart had, indeed, deceived him into believing almost *anything* but the gospel of Jesus Christ. I did not win him over to Christ, but I think I spoke the truth which he needed to hear.

You may be aware of the fact that God sustained His people Israel during their sojourn in the wilderness. He provided *manna*, a term which literally means, "What is it?" Jesus calls Himself the *manna* come down from heaven in John 6. Keenly conscious of why He had come to the earth, Jesus says, "I am the living bread that came down from heaven. If anyone eats of this bread, he will *live forever*. This bread is my flesh, which I will give for the life of the world" (6:51). Later He says, "Whoever eats my flesh and drinks my blood . . . will *live forever*" (6:54, 58). It is not surprising that the thousands who had been fed by Jesus in John 6 "voted with their feet" and forsook Jesus after these incredible claims!

When Christ uses the phrase, "whoever eats my flesh and drinks my blood," we should not be surprised that some opponents of the early Christian church thought that a form of cannibalism was being commanded by Jesus. The second-century Roman leader Pliny the Younger writes to Emperor Trajan for advice about how to deal with people suspected of being Christians, and Pliny refers to the meals that Christians had with each other. He tells us that the Christians met before daybreak, sang a hymn to Christ as to a god, and committed themselves to living with integrity and honesty. He then writes, "After the conclusion of this ceremony it was their custom to depart and meet again to take food; *but it was ordinary and harmless food. . . .*"[13] The early Christians were not engaging in cannibalism; they were commemorating the sacrifice of the One who had given them *life*!

The Good Shepherd and Role Reversal

Jesus warns us that, "The thief comes only to steal and kill and destroy; I have come that they may have life, and have it to the full" (10:10). Do we Christians visibly enjoy life "to the full"? I agree with the preacher who said, "Christians owe it to the world to be supernaturally joyful!" Sometimes followers of Christ walk around looking like they've been baptized in lemon juice. Christ did not come to bring abundant *death*, but abundant *life*.

In a culture accustomed to raising animals in order to sacrifice them to God, Jesus declares, "My sheep listen to my voice; I know them, and they follow me. I give them *eternal life*, and they shall never perish; no one can snatch them out of my hand" (10:27-28). Non-perishing sheep was indeed a unique concept. And instead of the shepherd offering His sheep for sacrifice, it is the *Shepherd* who would sacrifice Himself for the sheep, thereby giving them eternal life. Someone has rightly said, "Eternal life is the gift of Jesus Christ. And the hard reality is, if you don't have *Him*, you don't have *it*."

The Definition of "Eternal Life"

In His very personal prayer to His Father in John 17, the Lord Jesus not only speaks of how He would glorify the Father, but also of the *definition* of *eternal life*: "Father, the time has come. Glorify your Son, that your Son may glorify you. For you granted him authority over all people that he might give *eternal life* to all those you have given him. Now this is *eternal life*: that they may know you, the only true God, and Jesus Christ, whom you have sent" (17:1-3). Eternal life is not mere longevity; it is an intimate relationship with the Father and the Son!

The Bible teaches that eternal life is the *present possession* of the believer (10:28). It also teaches that the fullness of eternal life is a *future event*, in texts such as Mark 10:30 and Titus 1:2. If eternal life is intimacy with the Father and the Son, then this life should demonstrate growth in that relationship which will be brought to perfection in glory.

A Misnomer's Conversion

As we conclude our brief look at John's Gospel, we must not overlook the story of the man commonly called "Doubting Thomas." I think he really should be re-named "Adamantly Unbelieving Thomas," for the language he uses about his refusal to believe in the resurrected Christ goes way beyond mere doubt: "Unless I see the nail marks in his hands and put my finger where the nails were, and put my hand into his side, I will *by no means* believe it!" (20:25, author paraphrase). Jesus gives "Adamantly Unbelieving Thomas" a week for his words of unbelief to marinate in his mind, and then grants his request by appearing before him for a private conversation. Thomas loses all desire to empirically investigate the crucifixion wounds of Jesus, and responds to Christ's appearance with the most reasonable (and *scientific!*) statement: "My Lord and my God!" (20:28).

It appears to me that John's epilogue in 20:30-31 is referring back to this episode between Jesus and Thomas. John writes, "Jesus did many other miraculous signs in the presence of his disciples, which are not recorded in this book. But these are written that you may believe that Jesus is the Christ, the Son of God, and that by believing you may have *life* in his name."

What keeps an individual from receiving the divine gift of eternal life? *Unbelief!* Followers of Jesus Christ are to seek out the "Adamantly Unbelieving Thomases" of our generation and present the evidences for Christ to them.

A Summary Regarding Eternal Life

We have seen from our quick survey of John's Gospel that "eternal life" is not simply *longevity,* or the eternal extension of one's earthly life. It is a different *quality* of life ("life . . . more abundantly," 10:10, KJV). One who possesses eternal life will not *perish* (3:16). He is no longer under the wrath of God (3:36). He will never thirst (4:14). He has crossed over from death to life (5:24). He will be raised up on the last day (6:44). He has every reason to be supernaturally joyful

(7:38). He has the confidence that nothing can snatch him out of Christ's hand (10:28-30). John 17:6 declares that the believer is the gift of the Father to the Son. Every human being will either experience eternal life (through the redemptive work of Christ) or eternal death (because of unbelief; see Revelation 2:11; 20:6). So Christians need to get busy sharing the gospel. It really is a life-or-death issue.

The Urgency of Evangelism

"Do you believe in life after death?" the boss asked one of his employees.

"Yes, sir," the new recruit replied.

"Well, that makes sense," the boss went on, "because after you left early yesterday to go to your mother's funeral, she stopped in to see you."

Many people may say that they do not believe in life after death, but they are sadly mistaken. And to face death without Jesus Christ is the worst possible situation one can encounter.

While on his deathbed, H.G. Wells said, "Go away. I'm all right." But he wasn't "all right." If he entered eternity without Jesus Christ, he was all wrong! In a work entitled *Dear M: Letters from a Gentleman of Excess*, Jack Pollock writes, "I've been thinking of death a lot, and I am amazed by its inevitability, frightened, as we all are, of the totally unknown, and yet feel a long sleep is somehow earned by those of us who live on the edge." But what if it isn't just a "long sleep"?

The Great Omission[14]

The believer in Jesus Christ must become burdened for lost men and women. In the off-Broadway musical *The Fantasticks*, one song emphasizes our need to care for others: "Deep in December, it's nice to remember, without a hurt, the heart is hollow." As commentator Cal Thomas puts it, "The fact is, burdenless lives create superficial people whose only interest is themselves."[15] God is honored when our hearts become burdened for the lost.

Any theology which implies that we can overlook, minimize or edit the Great Commission of Matthew 28:18-20 is bogus. There we read Jesus' final instructions to His disciples:

> All authority in heaven and on earth has been given to me. Therefore go and make disciples of all nations, baptizing them in the name of the Father and of the Son and of the Holy Spirit, and teaching them to obey everything I have commanded you. And surely I am with you always, to the very end of the age.

Jesus' parable of the great banquet in Luke 14 indicates that those who were initially invited to the banquet made excuses for not coming. The owner became angry and ordered his servant to "Go out quickly into the streets and alleys of the town and bring in the poor, the crippled, the blind and the lame" (14:21). The servant obeys, but "there is still room," he tells his master (14:22). "Go out to the roads and country lanes and make them come in, so that my house will be full" (14:23). God wants His banquet FULL!

As a seminary professor I have to read a lot of religious opinions with which I clearly disagree. When it comes to the issue of heaven and hell, to the question of where people will spend eternity, a comment I recently read by the liberal theologian Delwin Brown really upset me. He writes,

> I understand persons to be essentially dynamic and relational. This means that judgment, and

the related imagery of heaven and hell, cannot apply to persons conceived as some one unchanging
"thing" or in isolation from their concrete con-
texts. This, in turn, means that isolated people
cannot "go" to some "place" called heaven or hell
rather like distinct apples can be assigned to baskets labeled "good or bad."[16]

But what about Jesus' parable of the weeds which will be
separated from the wheat at the end of time and burned at
the judgment (Matthew 13:24-30, 36-43)? Or His parable
about the good and bad fish in 13:47-50? There He says that
the "good fish" are put in baskets, but the "bad fish" are
thrown away. Jesus says, "This is how it will be at the end of
the age. The angels will come and separate the wicked from
the righteous and throw them into the fiery furnace, where
there will be weeping and gnashing of teeth" (13:49-50).

The issue is not what we "think" or what we "understand." If
the Bible is true, then we must submit our understanding,
which is conditioned by our sin and our circumstances, to God's
Word. And it does not hesitate to declare:

> The house of the wicked will be destroyed,
>   but the tent of the upright will flourish.
> There is a way that seems right to a man,
>   but in the end it leads to death.
>
> (Proverbs 14:11-12)

One of the primary ways that I can get ready for heaven
is to strive to not go there *alone*. Evangelism focuses my
heart on the lost and their destiny without Christ. The
second way I can get ready for heaven is best explained by
briefly discussing my youth.

The Priority of Personal Purity

When I was a young Christian, I recall a number of itinerant preachers coming through our small North Carolina town and preaching in our church. At that time (the '60s) the predominant theme in Christian circles was eschatology (the study of end-time events). Extended discussions of the pretribulational, premillennial Second Coming of Christ were vigorously presented, as well as challenging messages on the Judgment Seat of Christ, the Tribulation, Armaggedon, the Great White Throne Judgment, and the Eternal State (heaven and hell).

One preacher even had a multicolored banner which was strung from one wall to the other on the speaker's platform. It had the title "From Eternity to Eternity" and had pictures which told the biblical story from creation through the events depicted in the book of Revelation. A lot of fine material was presented by that preacher, but what I remember most was being confused about all the various events and thinking to myself, *I'll bet this sermon is going to last "From Eternity to Eternity"*!

There's been a lot of water under the bridge since then, and I now find myself teaching many of the same truths which bored me during my teenage years. I think what troubled me so much during that time was my belief that those preachers failed to make their prophetic studies *practical* to my life. They appeared to me to be engaged in much speculation and debate about issues that seemed to have no real present meaning.

One of the features of prophetic material in the Bible is that of practical and present application. For example, we read in Second Peter 3 about the final destruction of the old creation in God's judgment: "But the day of the Lord will come like a thief. The heavens will disappear with a roar; the elements will be destroyed by fire, and the earth and everything in it will be laid bare" (3:10).

Immediately Peter adds these words: "Since everything will be destroyed in this way, make sure you have given up your earthly jobs, dispossessed yourselves of all that you own, taken your children out of public school, and are waiting patiently in your ascension robes on the highest hill in the county for the glorious appearing of our Lord Jesus Christ."

Sorry, but I made up most of that previous sentence! Peter really says in verses 11 and 12: "Since everything will be destroyed in this way, what kind of people ought you to be? You ought to live holy and godly lives as you look forward to the day of God and speed its coming."

With our attention focused on earth's eventual destruction, one might think that we can sit back on our Christian laurels and do nothing but *wait*! But prophecy (God's announcement of future events) ought to spur us to present godliness.

The same idea comes out in First John 3:1-2 where John says,

> How great is the love the Father has lavished on us, that we should be called children of God! And that is what we are! The reason the world does not know us is that it did not know him. Dear friends, now we are children of God, and what we will be has not yet been made known. But we know that when he appears, we shall be like him, for we shall see him as he is.

John very quickly follows up this fantastic future certainty with a present challenge: "Everyone who has this hope in him purifies himself, just as he is pure" (3:3).

We read in James that "a double-minded man [is] unstable in all his ways" (James 1:8, NASB). The context in James concerns praying in faith for God's will. But is there not a sense in which the Christian can appropriately be "double-minded"? What I mean is that the Christian both focuses on the *next* world, but also seeks to become holy in *this* world. There is no room for a kind of Christian fatalism which says, "Well, this world is going to be burned up anyway. We might as well live as we please!" No, the certainty that God will judge this world provides the most reasonable foundation for us to advance in our holiness. Martin Luther was once asked what he would do if he knew Christ was coming back tomorrow. He said he would pay his bills and plant an apple tree!

Adrian Rogers tells the story of some gold prospectors who discovered an exceptionally rich mine. One of them said, "Hey, we've got it made as long as we don't tell anybody else before we stake our claims." So they each vowed to keep the secret. Because they had to have more tools and provisions, they headed for town. After buying all the supplies they needed, they hurried back to the mine site. But they weren't alone. A crowd of people followed them because their discovery was written all over their faces!

Our world desperately needs to see evidences of our longing for heaven on our faces—and in our lives. Donald Grey Barnhouse was teaching a group of young men how to preach on heaven and hell. He said, "Men, when you preach about heaven, let your face glow with the joy of that celestial place. And when you preach about hell, then your everyday face will do."

Conclusion

We began this book by saying that somebody has stolen heaven from the Christian. That theft has many facets, from those who suggest that we should imagine heaven away to those who foolishly claim to have taken tours of glory. Others have misidentified heaven, either treating this world as the only one or demanding all the blessings of God this side of eternity.

Although we have not examined every biblical passage on the subject of heaven, we have recognized that heaven came down in the person of the Incarnate Son of God, the Lord Jesus Christ. We have been given a few details about glory from one of God's servants who was hijacked to heaven. And we have been challenged to commit ourselves to evangelism and personal growth in godliness "for heaven's sake."

If this book has encouraged the Christian to long for his or her heavenly home, then it has accomplished its purpose. That longing must no longer be stifled or covered up by this world's poor substitutes. C.S. Lewis so eloquently challenges us,

> . . . it would seem that Our Lord finds our desires, not too strong, but too weak. We are half-hearted creatures, fooling about with drink and sex and ambition when infinite joy is offered us, like an ignorant child who wants to go on making mud pies in a slum because he cannot imagine what is meant by the offer of a holiday at the sea. We are far too easily pleased.[17]

May God grant each of us a divine discontent as we make all the preparations we can for that day—when we finally get home!

Endnotes

Introduction

1. Larry Dixon, *The Other Side of the Good News* (Wheaton, IL: BridgePoint, 1992).
2. J.B. Phillips, *Your God Is Too Small* (New York: Macmillan, 1961), pp. 15-18.
3. Ibid., pp. 23-26.

Chapter 1: Imagine There's No Heaven

1. Soundtrack from the movie *Footloose*, 1984.
2. Shania Twain, "You Win My Love," 1995.
3. Maria Shriver, *What's Heaven?* (Racine, WI: Golden Books, 1999). One Christian reviewer commented, "This book was easy to read. But, that's about the only good thing I can say about it. This book is a good example of the mysticism that is sweeping our country. This spiritual movement allows people to feel good about themselves without having to acknowledge a real God. This book gives kids some comfort when a loved one dies; some would say, 'then it must be good.' I say, it might comfort a child to assure them that their house isn't on fire; but if their house is on fire, you have done them a grave misservice. This book assures kids that if you are a 'good' person then you will go to Heaven. This is a fine idea, and it is comforting. The only problem is that nobody can be good—according to the Bible (that's the whole reason Jesus came). This book is comforting, but we must realize that our house is on fire and there is only one way to escape . . . Jesus. This book leads children to death" (titus3five@hotmail.com, July 4, 1999).
4. John Lennon, "Imagine," 1971.
5. "The Last Day in the Life: John Lennon (1940-1980)," *Time* Magazine, December 22, 1980.
6. Available online at www.antichrist.com/lennon.htm
7. Ibid.
8. Blaise Pascal, *Pascal's Pensées* (New York: E.P. Dutton, 1958), p. 67.
9. Ibid. Italics in original.
10. Ibid., p. 68.
11. Ibid.

12. Charles Colson (with Nancy R. Pearcey), *A Dangerous Grace: Daily Readings* (Dallas: Word Publishing, 1994), pp. 80-81.
13. Paul Johnson, quoted in Colson, *A Dangerous Grace*, p. 12.
14. Larry Dixon, "Don't Worry!", *Moody* Magazine, July-August, 1998.

Chapter 2: Hijacked to Paradise

1. C.S. Lewis, *The Great Divorce* (New York: The Macmillan Company, 1946). This novel has nothing to do with the institution of marriage—although I know of one college student who included it in a research paper on the subject of marriage and divorce!
2. Ibid., pp. 72-73.
3. For further discussion of this passage, note pages 130-144 in Dixon, *The Other Side of the Good News*.
4. Clark H. Pinnock and Delwin Brown, *Theological Crossfire: An Evangelical/Liberal Dialogue* (Grand Rapids: Zondervan, 1990), p. 224.
5. Eugene H. Peterson, *The Message: The New Testament, Psalms and Proverbs* (Colorado Springs: NavPress, 1993), p. 387.
6. William Barclay, *The Daily Study Bible: The Letters to the Corinthians* (Toronto: G.R. Welch Co., 1975), p. 256.
7. C.S. Lewis, *The Great Divorce*, pp. 106-107.
8. C.S. Lewis, *The Screwtape Letters* (New York: The Macmillan Company, 1961), p. 102.
9. William F. Arndt and F. Wilbur Gingrich, *A Greek-English Lexicon of the New Testament and Other Early Christian Literature* (Chicago, The University of Chicago Press, 1957), **arrētos**, p. 109.
10. Ibid., **harpazō**, p. 108.
11. Ibid., **optasia**, p. 580.
12. W. Harold Mare, "The New Testament Concept Regarding the Regions of Heaven with Emphasis on 2 Corinthians 12:1-4," *Grace Theological Journal*, Winter, 1970, vol. 11, No. 1, p. 9.

Chapter 3: Wrong Thoughts of Heaven

1. Available online at http://www.he.net/~mousel/denver.html.
2. Available online at http://www.sonymusic.com/artists/JohnDenver/bio.html.
3. "Late Greats," an obituary for John Denver, *Life* Magazine, January 1998, p. 122.
4. Available online at http://www.sonymusic.com/artists/JohnDenver/bio.html.
5. Richard Lacayo, "Cult of Death," *Time* Magazine, May 22, 1993.

6. Malcolm Muggeridge, *Jesus Rediscovered* (New York: Doubleday & Co., 1979), pp. 17-18.

7. Quoted in David Smith, *A Handbook of Contemporary Theology* (Wheaton: Victor Books, 1992), p. 197.

8. Ibid.

9. David W. Jones, "The Bankruptcy of the Prosperity Gospel: An Exercise in Biblical and Theological Ethics," *Faith & Mission*, Vol. 16, No. 1, Fall, 1998, p. 81, quoting from Copeland's book *The Troublemaker* (Fort Worth: Kenneth Copeland Publications, 1996).

10. Ibid., p. 87 (from Tilton's TBN program of Dec. 27, 1990).

11. *The Winnipeg Free Press*, August 22, 1992.

12. Ibid.

13. Ibid.

14. Jim Bakker with Ken Abraham, *I Was Wrong* (Nashville: Thomas Nelson, 1996), p. 532.

15. Ibid., pp. 534-5.

16. Ibid., p. 543.

17. C.S. Lewis, *Screwtape Letters*, p. 132.

18. Quoted in Os Guinness, *The Dust of Death* (Downers Grove, IL: InterVarsity, 1973), p. 40.

19. B.F. Skinner, *Beyond Freedom and Dignity* (New York: Alfred A. Knopf, 1971), p. 215.

20. *Letter to Diognetes*, c. A.D. 150. Cited in Philip Schaff, *History of the Christian Church*, Vol. II, "Ante-Nicene Christianity" (Grand Rapids: Eerdmans Publishing Co., 1910), p. 9.

21. Our discussion of heaven and animals in Chapter 6 reflects on this issue.

22. C.S. Lewis, "On Living in an Atomic Age," *Present Concerns: Essays by C.S. Lewis*, ed. Walter Hooper (New York: Harcourt Brace Jovanovich, 1986), p. 79.

23. C.S. Lewis, *Mere Christianity* (New York: Macmillan, 1952), Bk. 3, ch. 10.

24. C.S. Lewis, "Some Thoughts," *The First Decade*, cited in *A Mind Awake: An Anthology of C.S. Lewis* (New York: Harcourt, Brace & World, 1968), p. 141.

Chapter 4: Heaven Only Knows!

1. Please be assured that the story which follows, as well as my claim to a special ability, is pure fiction, completely in jest!

2. G. Richard Fisher, "Heaven Hopping . . . Spirituality, Sensational-
   ism or Spiritism?" *Personal Freedom Outreach* Newsletter, Oct.-Dec.
   1985, vol. 5, no. 4, p. 4.

3. Ibid., p. 6.

4. Ibid.

5. Mary K. Baxter, *A Divine Revelation of Hell* (New Kensington, PA:
   Whitaker House, 1993) and *A Divine Revelation of Heaven* (New
   Kensington, PA: Whitaker House, 1998).

6. *A Divine Revelation of Heaven*, p. 13.

7. *A Divine Revelation of Hell*, p. 17.

8. *A Divine Revelation of Heaven*, p. 9.

9. *A Divine Revelation of Hell*, pp. 61-62.

10. *A Divine Revelation of Heaven*, p. 144.

11. See both *A Divine Revelation of Hell*, p. 2 and *A Divine Revelation of
    Heaven*, p. 143.

12. *A Divine Revelation of Hell*, pp. 96-97.

13. Ibid., p. 65.

14. Ibid., pp. 112, 174, 185.

15. Ibid., pp. 41-43.

16. Ibid., p. 72.

17. Ibid., p. 97.

18. Ibid., p. 148.

19. Ibid., pp. 108-109.

20. *A Divine Revelation of Heaven*, p. 209, as cited in G. Richard Fisher's
    "Mary Baxter's Vision of Hell: Divine Revelation or Deluded
    Ranting?", *The Quarterly Journal*, Oct.-Dec. 1995, vol. 15, no. 5, p.
    15. In another article Fisher points out that this idea of angelic scru-
    tiny "is akin to the progressive salvation and the 'investigative judg-
    ment' of Ellen G. White and the Adventists" (G. Richard Fisher,
    "The Heavenly Hash of Mary K. Baxter: A Critical Look at Her Ce-
    lestial Revelation," *The Quarterly Journal*, Jan.-March 1999, vol. 19,
    no. 1, p. 17).

21. *A Divine Revelation of Heaven*, p. 113.

22. Ibid., pp. 54-55.

23. Fisher, "Mary Baxter's Vision of Hell: Divine Revelation or Deluded
    Ranting?", p. 14.

24. See my article on the wrath of God, "Warning a Wrath-Deserving
    World: Evangelicals and the Overhaul of Hell," *The Emmaus Jour-
    nal*, Vol. 2, No. 1, Summer 1993, pp. 7-21.

25. *A Divine Revelation of Hell*, p. 37.

26. Fisher, "Mary Baxter's Vision of Hell . . .", p. 15.
27. A *Divine Revelation of Heaven*, pp. 54-55.
28. Ibid., p. 56.
29. Ibid., p. 87.
30. Ibid., p. 90.
31. Fisher, "The Heavenly Hash of Mary K. Baxter . . .", p. 19.
32. Ibid., pp. 19-20.
33. Ibid., p. 20.
34. Ibid., p. 19.
35. Ibid., p. 20.
36. Fisher, "The Heavenly Hash of Mary K. Baxter . . .", p. 17.
37. A.W. Tozer, *That Incredible Christian* (Camp Hill, PA: Christian Publications, 1964), p. 82.
38. A.W. Tozer, *Man, the Dwelling Place of God* (Camp Hill, PA: Christian Publications, 1966, 1997), p. 138.
39. A *Divine Revelation of Heaven*, pp. 123ff.
40. *The Quarterly Journal: The Newsletter Publication of Personal Freedom Outreach*, Jan-March 1999, vol. 19, No. 1.
41. William Alnor, *Heaven Can't Wait: A Survey of Alleged Trips to the Other Side* (Grand Rapids: Baker, 1996).
42. Fisher, "Mary Baxter's Vision of Hell . . .", p. 1.
43. Fisher, "The Heavenly Hash of Mary K. Baxter . . .", p. 17.
44. Fisher, "Mary Baxter's Vision of Hell . . .", p. 16.

Chapter 6: Heaven Came Down

1. *Worship Hymn II*, compiled by Jessie Peterson and Bruce Ballinger (1989, Tempo Music Publications, distributed by Alexandria House; song is copyright 1989 Sound III Inc., Leawood, Kansas). No known composer.
2. Arndt and Gingrich, A *Greek-English Lexicon . . .*, **geuomai**, p. 156.
3. Robert H. Stein, *Luke*. From *The New American Commentary* Series, Volume 24 (Nashville: Broadman Press, 1992), p. 280.
4. Ibid.
5. Arndt and Gingrich, A *Greek-English Lexicon . . .*, **metamorphoō**, p. 513.
6. Ibid.
7. Ibid., **gnapheus**, p. 162.
8. Ibid., **stilbō**, p. 776.
9. Ibid., **anēr, andros**, pp. 65-66.
10. Ibid., **horaō**, pp. 581-582.

11. Ibid., **exodos,** p. 276.
12. Stein, *Luke*, pp. 284-285.
13. Arndt and Gingrich, *A Greek-English Lexicon* . . . , **diaxōrizō,** p. 190.
14. Stein, *Luke*, p. 169.
15. Arndt and Gingrich, *A Greek-English Lexicon* . . . , **skēnē,** p. 762.
16. E.J. Tinsley, *The Gospel According to Luke*. From *The Cambridge Bible Commentary on the New English Bible* (Cambridge: The University Press, 1965), p. 104.
17. Stein, *Luke*, p. 285.
18. David Gooding, *According to Luke: A New Exposition of the Third Gospel* (Grand Rapids: Eerdmans, 1987), p. 169.
19. Stein, *Luke*, p. 285.
20. Arndt and Gingrich, *A Greek-English Lexicon* . . . , **phōteinos,** p. 880.
21. Gooding, *According to Luke*, p. 167.
22. Ibid.

Chapter 7: Endless Inactivity?

1. Arndt and Gingrich, *A Greek-English Lexicon* . . ., **stenazō,** p. 773.
2. Ibid., **bareō,** p. 133.
3. C.S. Lewis, *Mere Christianity*, Bk. 3, ch. 5, p. 91.
4. Leo Aikman in the *Atlanta Constitution*.
5. Charles Ryrie, *Basic Theology* (Wheaton: Victor Books, 1988), pp. 512ff.
6. Wayne Grudem, *Systematic Theology: An Introduction to Biblical Doctrine* (Grand Rapids: Zondervan, 1994), pp. 1141-1142.
7. Nels F.S. Ferré, *The Christian Understanding of God* (London: SCM Press, 1951), p. 237.
8. Larry Dixon, *The Other Side of the Good News*, discusses universalism in detail in Chapter 3.
9. Craig L. Blomberg, "Degrees of Rewards in the Kingdom of Heaven" *Journal of the Evangelical Theological Society*, Vol. 35, no. 2, June 1992, pp. 159-172.
10. Ibid., p. 161.
11. Ibid., pp. 161-162.
12. Ibid., p. 162.
13. Ibid.
14. Ibid., pp. 162-163.
15. Ibid., p. 163.
16. Ibid.
17. Ibid.

18. Ibid., p. 165.
19. Ibid.
20. Ibid.
21. Ibid., p. 167.
22. Ibid.
23. Ibid., p. 168.
24. Ibid., p. 169.
25. Ibid.
26. Mary Buddemeyer-Porter, *Will I See Fido in Heaven?: Scripturally Revealing God's Eternal Plan for His Lesser Creatures* (Shippensburg, PA: Companion Press, 1995), "About This Book."
27. Ibid., p. 1.
28. Ibid., p. 77.
29. Ibid., p. 37.
30. Ibid., p. 87.
31. Ibid., p. 21.
32. Ibid., p. 17.
33. Ibid., p. 20.
34. Ibid., p. 21.
35. Ibid., pp. 6-7.
36. Ibid., p. 3.
37. Ibid., p. 5.
38. Ibid., pp. 9-10.
39. Ibid., pp. 19-20.
40. Ibid., p. 40.
41. Ibid., "Introduction."
42. Ibid., pp. 12-13.
43. Ibid., p. 71.
44. Ibid., p. 21.
45. Ibid., p. 88.
46. Ibid., p. 3.
47. Ibid., p. 75.
48. Ibid., p. 61.
49. Ibid., p. 62.
50. Ibid., p. 72.
51. Ibid., p. 91.
52. Ibid., p. 88.
53. Ibid., p. 92.
54. Ibid., p. 85.
55. Ibid., pp. 85-86.

56. Ibid.
57. Julian Huxley, *Religion without Revelation* (New York: New American Library, 1957).
58. Quoted in Dixon, *The Other Side of the Good News*, p. 152. [Jonathan Edwards, "A Treatise Concerning Religious Affections," in *The Works of Jonathan Edwards*, Vol. 2, ed. Perry Miller (New Haven: Yale University Press, 1957).]
59. C.S. Lewis, *Mere Christianity*, Bk. 1, ch. 5, p. 38.
60. James W. Sire, *The Universe Next Door: A Basic World View Catalog* (Downers Grove, IL: InterVarsity, 1976), p. 42.
61. Cynthia Heald, "Becoming a Friend of God," *Discipleship Journal*, Nov./Dec. 1989, vol. 9, no. 6, issue 54, p. 27.
62. *Faith at Work*, Jan/Feb 1993, p. 3.

Chapter 8: For Heaven's Sake!

1. Available at <http:\\www.ag.wastholm.net\author\John_Barrymore>
2. *World* Magazine, April 3, 1999, p. 14.
3. See my book, *The Other Side of the Good News*, pp. 121-147.
4. John E. Sanders, "Is Belief in Christ Necessary for Salvation?", *Evangelical Quarterly* 60 (1988), p. 245.
5. "You Should Live So Long," *Time* Magazine, November 12, 1990, p. 86.
6. Ibid. The Bible, however, implies that man's fall dramatically shortened his life.
7. "How to Live to Be 120," *Time* Magazine, March 6, 1995, p. 85. Chuck Colson writes, "There's a new American fad that comes from ancient Egypt: People are signing up to have their bodies turned into mummies when they die. So far about 140 mummy-wannabes have put money down with a Utah-based company. The owner of the mummy company says his clients don't want to be 'covered with dirt and forgotten' "(Charles W. Colson with Nancy R. Pearcey, *A Dangerous Grace: Daily Readings*, p. 28). They want to be remembered after death to live on in some way. Apparently even thoroughly modern Americans still experience longings for eternity.
8. Pico Iyer, "Death Be Not a Stranger," *Time* Magazine, August 8, 1994, p. 68.
9. *Parade Magazine*, February 1, 1998, p. 20.
10. Available online at http://members.aol.com/BorrowTyme/quote.html.
11. Story related in the *Denver Post*.
12. Colson, *A Dangerous Grace*, p. 26.

13. *Letters of Pliny*, cited in F.F. Bruce, *Jesus and Christian Origins Outside the New Testament* (Grand Rapids: Eerdmans, 1974), p. 26. Emphasis mine.

14. I have borrowed this section heading from the book *The Great Omission: A Biblical Basis for World Evangelism* by Robertson McQuilkin (Grand Rapids: Baker Book House, 1984), a work which will challenge every Christian to get serious about sharing the gospel with the world.

15. Cal Thomas, *The Things That Matter Most* (Grand Rapids: Zondervan, 1994), p. 145.

16. Clark H. Pinnock and Delwin Brown, *Theological Crossfire: An Evangelical/Liberal Dialogue* (Grand Rapids: Zondervan, 1991), p. 246.

17. C.S. Lewis, *The Weight of Glory and Other Addresses* (New York: Macmillan, 1949), pp. 19-20.

Scripture Index

Old Testament

Genesis

1:1 67
2:15 49
2:3 75
3:22 68
5 68
5:24 68
14:19 67
19:24 69
22:11 68
22:15 68
28:17 68

Exodus

13:21 97
20:11 67
23:16 97
24:10 71
31:17 67
34:22 97

Leviticus

23:33-43 97
23:42-44 96

Deuteronomy

4 70
4:26 71
4:32 73
4:36 70
10:14 70
11:11 69
11:17 69
11:21 73

16:13-16 97
29:29 59
30:19 71
31:28 71
33:26 72

First Samuel

2:10 70

Second Samuel

12:23 75
22:8 70

First Kings

8:27 74
8:35 69

Second Kings

2:1 68

First Chronicles

21:16 70

Second Chronicles

7:14 70

Nehemiah

9:6 67

Job

11:7-9 72
20:27 71
22:12 72
26:2 72
26:11 72
38:33 72
38:37-38 72

Psalms

8:3-4 72-73
16:11 ....4, 134-135
17:15 66
19:1 73
20:6 73
23:6 76
31:17 66
41:11 111
65:13 129
69:34 71
78:23-25 69
88:10-12 66
98:8 129
102:25 73
103:11 74
104:35 66
105:40 69
108:4 74
115:16 70
115:17 66
119:89 74
123:1 76
137:8-9 115
139:8 74
143:3 66
148:13 73

Proverbs

3:5-6 115
14:11-12 162
14:12 7
25:3 70
30:24-28 129

Ecclesiastes

1:13 70
5:2 70

Isaiah

14 71
14:8 129
14:12 70-71
49:13 71
51:6 75
55:9 74
55:12 129
65:17 75
66:1 ....69, 74

Jeremiah

9:23-24 ....133, 149
17:9 156
23:24 74
31:37 74
33:25-26 74-75
51:15 67
51:48 71

Daniel

4:37 73
5:23 73
7:13 73
7:13-14 98
12:2 75-76

Amos

9:6 69

New Testament

Matthew

3:12 114
5:3 77
5:10 77
5:13-14 51
5:19 119

5:34..76
6:9..76
6:20..76, 123
 8:12 ....114, 124, 150
10:15...118
11:11...119
11:22...118
11:24...118
12:36...123
12:37...123
12:31-32 130
13:24-30 162
13:36-43 162
13:42...124
13:47-50 162
13:49-50 162
13:50...124
16:1-4 14
16:19...76
16:28.....................................141, 142
17:2...91, 92
17:2-9 89
17:3...93
17:4...95
17:5...99
17:6...99
18:4...119
19:16...123
19:21...123
19:23...123
19:23-24 77
20:1-16 118
22..116
22:13...124
22:29-32 117
24:35...76
24:51 ....124, 150

25..78
25:14-30............................12, 124
25:30...124
25:34.......................................78, 139
25:41.......................................78, 139
25:46.......................................78, 114
26:64...98
28:18-20 161

Mark

3:28-29 130
9:2..91
9:2-10 89
9:3..92
9:34-35 119
10:30...................................43, 158
10:35-45 124
10:40...124

Luke

9:22...89
9:25...90
9:26...90
9:27 ....90, 91
9:28...91
9:28-36 89
9:29...91, 92
9:30-31 93
9:31.....................93, 94, 100, 106
9:32...94
9:33 95-96
9:35...99
9:48...119
10:30-37 25
12 ....145, 147
12:2-3 123
12:19...146

12:20..147
12:21..148
12:35-48 12
12:47-48 118
13:18-19 25
14:16-24 25
14:21..161
14:22..161
14:23 ....3, 161
15:10..3
16 ....14, 25, 62
16:1-4 14
16:1-8 25
16:9..96, 97
16:19-31 ....23, 60, 109
16:26..24
16:28 ....24, 142
16:29-31 24
19:11-27................................12, 124
21:27..98
23:43..33

John

1:14 ....87, 94, 95
1:32..79
1:51 78-79
3 ....57, 78
3:13..78
3:16 ....115, 152, 159
3:18..151
3:31..78
3:36................59, 115, 150, 153, 159
4:14..153, 159
4:23..4
5:24..153, 159
5:39-40 154
6..78

6:27..155
6:32-33 78
6:33..155
6:38..78
6:40..155
6:42..78
6:44..159
6:51..156
6:54, 58 156-157
7:38..153, 160
7:39..153
8:21..141
8:24..20, 141
8:51..141, 142
10:10..157, 159
10:18..94
10:27-28 157-158
10:28..158
10:28-30 160
11 ....25, 60
11:4..142, 143
11:11..142
11:12..142
11:14..142
11:15..142
11:25-26 143
11:40..143
11:45..143
14 ....17, 57
14:1..18
14:1-3 ....10-11, 12, 47, 50, 69
14:2-3..79, 106
17..158
17:1-3 ....130-131, 158
17:6..160
17:17..53
18:36..37, 41

20:25...159
20:28...159
20:30-31 159

Acts

1:3...14
1:11 ....3, 79
2:28...79
3:19-21 79
7:60...142
8:39...33
10...79
10:11..79
12:2...95
26...33

Romans

1:4...17
12:2 91-92
2:6...123
2:7...123
5:13...118
8:1...60
8:18-23 107
8:20-21 129
14:10.....................................83, 113

First Corinthians

2:9 58-59
3:10...121
3:10-15..................113, 119, 120-121
3:11...121
3:12...121
3:13 121-122
3:14...122
3:15...122
4:6...59
6:1-4 125

9:25...119
13:12 ....106, 113, 118
15..109
15:5-9 15
15:14...15
15:15...15
15:17...15
15:18...15
15:19 14-15
15:32...15
15:47...78
15:49...79
15:54-57 150

Second Corinthians

1:22 108-109
3:18...91
5 ....100, 110, 112
5:1...106
5:2...106
5:3...106
5:4 106-107
5:5...108
5:6...110
5:6-9 ....29-30, 109
5:6-10 109
5:8...110
5:9 110-111
5:11...139
5:10 ....83, 112, 113
11:5...27
11:13...27
11:16-29 27
11:30...27
12...........................26, 27, 31, 32
12:1..........................31, 32, 33, 34
12:1-4 170

12:1-6 26
12:2 ....27, 29, 31, 32
12:2-4 21
12:3-4 ....27, 29
12:4 ....27, 31, 32, 33
12:5 27
12:6 27
12:7-10 28
12:7 ....28, 31, 33
12:7-9 60

Galatians

1:8 27
6:10 51

Ephesians

1:13-14 109
1:17 136
2:1-5 152
2:2 71
3:14-19 ....136, 152
4:30 109

Philippians

1:20-26 ....30, 109
2 88
3:21 127
3:11 124
3:14 124

Colossians

1:10-12 111
3:1 133

First Thessalonians

2:19 ....119, 120
4:17 98
4:17-18 103

5:9 60

First Timothy

1:3-4 64
6:19 123

Second Timothy

4:8 ....119, 120

Titus

1:2 158
2 46
2:12 46

Hebrews

11 47
11:1-2 47
11:10 47
11:13, 16 47-48
11:22 93
11:25-27 48
11:35 48
11:37 48
11:39-40 48-49
12:29 134

James

1:8 165
1:12 ....119, 120
4:14 140

First Peter

1:10-11 94
1:17 45
1:18-19 45
1:19 129
2:11-12 45-46
4:10 49

5:4 ....119, 120

Second Peter

1:15 93
1:16 ....87, 94
1:17-18 95
3 164
3:10 164
3:11-12 164

First John

1:5 135
2:28 122
3:1-2 164-165
3:1-3 2
3:2 ....4, 66, 80, 105, 137
3:3 ....3, 165
4:8, 16 134

Jude

7 114
23 33

Revelation

1:3 80
1:5-6 83
1:7 98
2:7 ....33, 80
2:10 83
2:11 160
2:17 80
2:26 83
3:5 80
3:9 83
3:11 83
3:12 81
3:21 84
4 62

4:8 32
4:10 120
4:10-11 83
5:5-6 80
5:8-9 81
5:9-10 84
5:11-12 81
5:13 ....81, 104
5:13-14 104
6:4 82
6:8 82
6:11 80
6:12 82
6:15-16 82
7:9 80
7:14 ....81, 92
7:17 116
8:5 82
9:20-21 82
11:18 115
12:7 82
13:6 96
14:2-3 81
15:2-3 81
16:9 82
16:11 82
16:21 82
18:22 81
19 79
19:7, 9 80
19:11 79
19:20 82
20:1-3 82
20:4 84
20:5-6 84
20:6 160
20:7-10 82

20:10...114
20:10-15 150
20:11-15...................................82, 113
20:14...82
20:15 ....115, 116
21-22 119
21:1..84
21:3..96
21:4..83
21:8..82
21:11..84
21:18..84
21:21..84
21:22-23 84
21:25..84
21:27..84
22:1..84
22:5..84
22:7..80
22:12..123
22:14 ....84, 123
22:15..82
22:17..84

Other Books by Larry Dixon

DocTALK
DocDEVOs
www.docdevos.com